In the Bosom of the Father

In the Bosom of the Father

The Collected Poems of a Benedictine Mystic

Swāmī Abhishiktānanda

Translated from the French by
Jacob Riyeff

Foreword by
Cyprian Consiglio

Afterword by
Swāmī Ātmānanda Udāsīn

RESOURCE *Publications* · Eugene, Oregon

IN THE BOSOM OF THE FATHER
The Collected Poems of a Benedictine Mystic

Copyright © 2018 Wipf and Stock. All rights reserved. Except for brief quotations in critical publications or reviews, no part of this book may be reproduced in any manner without prior written permission from the publisher. Write: Permissions, Wipf and Stock Publishers, 199 W. 8th Ave., Suite 3, Eugene, OR 97401.

Resource Publications
An Imprint of Wipf and Stock Publishers
199 W. 8th Ave., Suite 3
Eugene, OR 97401

www.wipfandstock.com

PAPERBACK ISBN: 978-1-5326-4020-9
HARDCOVER ISBN: 978-1-5326-4021-6
EBOOK ISBN: 978-1-5326-4022-3

Manufactured in the U.S.A.

The poems of Swāmī Abhishiktānanda are published with the permission of the Abhishiktānanda Center for Interreligious Dialogue (Delhi Brotherhood Society).

For Mamie

"*Écrire? Pour cet au-delà, la théologie ne suffit plus,
il faut la poésie ou son équivalent. Il faut l'inspiration au sens le plus fort. . . .
C'est trop fort de se sentir en presence du Vrai,
et comment dire en mots ce que les mots ne peuvent que trahir?*"

"To write? For this which is beyond, theology does not suffice,
poetry or its equivalent is needed. There is need of inspiration in its fullest
sense. . . .
It is too overpowering to feel oneself in the presence of the True,
and how can one express in words that which words would only betray?"

—Swāmī Abhishiktānanda
Letter to Odette Baumer-Despeigne
May 22, 1973

"*Nimirum, inuisibilis conditoris species,
repressa omni corporae uisionis imagine, in cubili cordis inuenitur.*"

"Without a doubt, the appearance of the invisible Creator,
without any image of bodily appearance,
is found there in the chamber of the heart."

—St. Gregory the Great
Morlia in Iob 8.24.41

Contents

Foreword by Cyprian Consiglio | xi
Preface and Acknowledgments | xxiii

Introduction | 1

Guhāntara: In the Heart of Arunāchala
(Contents according to the collection of 1968)

Arunāchala | 23
Poems Inspired by Tamil Verses | 31
Bhairava | 33
Beyond the Depths | 38
The Other Shore | 42
    1. *Ascent to the Source* | 42
    2. *Excerpts from the Upanishads* | 46
    3. *The Other Shore* | 47
    4. *(Awakening) In the Bosom of the Father* | 58
Shrī Ramana was Great | 61

Poems on Arunāchala by Shrī Ramana Maharshi and Adapted into French by Swāmī Abhishiktānanda
(Originally integrated into the collection of 1960)

The Nuptial Garland | 69
The Crown of Sixteen Diamonds | 89
Nine Gems | 97
Five Rubies | 99
Ulladu Narpadu I | 101
Shrī Ramana Gītā II.2 | 102

Praise in Truth | 103
The Way of Being | 105

Poems from the Diary of Swāmī Abhishiktānanda

In silence you teach me silence | 110
O Arunāchala | 111
I am not this | 114
Offer this moment as an Offering | 116
This life in the Depths | 117
Discover at the center of the self | 118
Within the depths | 119
Beyond the Depths | 120
Departure from Arunāchala | 121
Renounce my God | 123
Seek God until you find him beyond | 124
If I am, how can You be? | 125
The awakening to Jesus's being | 126
I will sing a song for my beloved | 127
I came here to make you known | 129
The mystery I carry within | 130
In serene solitude, in sovereign solitude | 131
But when Christ came to earth | 132
Advaita is when one has plunged into the guhā | 135
In this darkness | 136
If I want something | 137
Everything is his mūrti | 138
Salvation is in accepting the complete "Otherness" of God | 140
And sometimes you are called to sing | 141
You will only become yourself | 142
To be one with You, Lord | 143
I am from God | 144
Faith is the psyche's gloaming | 145
In the depth of myself | 146
Jesus was pure, perfectly pure | 147
I no longer saw you | 148
As long as you approach Christ | 149
See everything as Jesus did | 150
Pass through what passes | 151

Contents

You have seen the lightning | 152
If there is no you | 154
Waiting for God | 155
Who are you, Lord? | 156
Feel in myself Jesus issuing from himself | 158
In the light of the ātman | 160
The Trinity is a three-fold depth | 163
This experience of intimacy | 164
You are | 165
A meeting this week with very sincere preachers of Christ | 166

Poems and Poetic Passages from Other Prose Sources

From "Cheminements intérieurs" | 171
It is, then | 173
From "Ehieh asher ehieh" | 174
From "L'Epiphanie de Dieu" | 176
If this body is allowed to drop away | 180
In my greatest depths | 182
And I also sing the OM | 183
In the Gospel | 185
ॐ *Wholly burnt* | 186
Easter joy! | 188
ॐ *Dear child* | 189
I wrote my monastery to say "Hallelujah" | 190
You a baby? | 191
OM Marc | 192
MARC | 197
Now the last sign itself is over | 198

Afterword by Swāmī Ātmānanda Udāsīn | 199

   Glossary | 205
   Appendix | 217
   Books by Swāmī Abhishiktānanda (chronologically by first publication in English) | 221
   Further Reading (in English) | 223
   Bibliography | 225

Foreword

WHEN I FIRST JOINED monastic life, almost everyone in my community had read something by, or knew something about, Swāmī Abhishiktānanda. For me, a typical Midwestern American cradle Catholic, even though I had already been immersed in the environs of religious life for significant periods, everything from the exotic sound of his Sanskrit name to the discussions about advaita/non-duality and the *sannyāsa* mendicant monastic tradition of India was a new world and the unfurling of a hitherto undreamt-of dimension to and possible expression of Christian spirituality.

My own Benedictine congregation, the Camaldolese, takes certain ownership of Swāmī Abhishiktānanda. His successor at Saccidānanda Āshram (Shāntivanam), which Swāmī Abhishiktānanda founded with Père Jules Monchanin, was Bede Griffiths, an Oxford-educated English Benedictine and an intimate friend of C. S. Lewis. After years of exclaustration from his own Prinknash Abbey in the Cotswalds of England, Fr. Bede brought himself and the monks of the āshram under the protection of our congregation in 1983, and so Shāntivanam is now a Camaldolese community, which I have visited numerous times. Swāmī Abhishiktānanda's remains were transferred to the cemetery there next to Bede's and a memorial to Monchanin. Whenever I was at Shāntivanam, each morning after prayers I would join several others singing a *bhajan* in honor of the gurus at the graves.

I had the great privilege of meeting Fr. Bede during his last trip to America in 1992. (He died back in India the following May.) He spent several days with us and gave a chapter conference at the end of the week. I often recount that that conference was a seminal moment in my spiritual journey, and the one that certainly set the tone of my own monastic life. In that one encounter Bede opened up that new world to me, offering me a new vision of reality (to quote one of his own book titles) and introducing me to a new language for articulating the Christian religious experience.

These last two elements strike me as the most important —experience and language, a new language for articulating the Christian religious experience, perhaps a new depth experience of Christianity.

After that experience with Fr. Bede, I delved deeply into Bede's own writings on universal wisdom and interreligious dialogue, which of course led me to Swāmī Abhishiktānanda, all of whose writings I eventually absorbed as well. As a matter of fact, I believe I have re-read his book *The Further Shore*, his essay on *sannyāsa* with an introduction to the Upanishads, nearly every time I have been in India.

Bede and Swāmī Abhishiktānanda were two very different personalities, and most folks who have read both have a strong preference for one or the other. Having met several people who knew them both, I can safely say that they didn't seem to enjoy each other's company all that much. While himself writing in a very prophetic way exploring the limits of Christian philosophical and theological assumptions, Bede was very measured in his writings. Apparently at one point Swāmī Abhishiktānanda referred to him as "the fog of the Thames." Bede, on the other hand, referred to Swāmī Abhishiktānanda as a "fiery Breton" and hinted that he thought the other had gone too far.[1] Swāmī Abhishiktānanda's experience of oneness with God while in a cave on the mountain of Arunāchala in Tiruvannamalai was in fact so profound that it "shook his faith in the traditional form of Christianity," Bede wrote with uncharacteristic frankness. In his experience of *advaita*, Swāmī Abhishiktānanda was left with a sense of absolute oneness in which he no longer felt any difference between God and the individual human person. For the rest of his life, as evidenced in his diaries, Swāmī Abhishiktānanda had to wrestle with how to interpret this experience as a Christian. It seemed to involve a denial of the "rational difference between God and creation, whereas his Christian faith called for the recognition of distinctions in the Godhead and the Incarnation and the church."[2]

And so we are back once again to experience and language —how first of all to understand it, and then how to express this experience, let alone be transformed by it. How many songs have been written about

---

1. Du Boulay, *The Cave of the Heart*, 154 and Fr. Francis Mahieu in personal communication with foreword author, 2000.

2. Griffiths, "Our Founders," 7–8.

the experience of falling in love, and yet do any of them ever fully capture it? Jesus himself in the gospels never says exactly what the reign of God is in all its dimensions. Rather, he speaks in parables: the kingdom of God is like a pearl of great price, like yeast in the dough, like a mustard seed.

But we must never forget that the transformative experience itself, undoubtedly, is the most important factor. As Swāmī Abhishiktānanda wrote in a letter toward the end of his life, "Of course I can make use of Christ's experience to lead Christians to an 'I AM' experience, yet it is this I AM experience which really matters."[3]

The original inspiration of Christianity, obviously, is Jesus, who articulated that experience according to his own background and that of his listeners, as a Palestinian Jew steeped in the Torah (the Law), the Prophets, and the language of the psalms. By the time that *kerygma* is being first written down, starting some thirty years after Jesus' death and resurrection, there is already a bit of a "spin" being put on the story, if you will. Certainly each of the Gospel writers has a particular audience in mind —Matthew is preaching to Jewish converts, Luke more to Gentiles, for example. St. Paul borrows from many sources to try to articulate the Gospel, particularly to people who have been steeped in Hellenistic thought, both Gentiles and Jews of the diaspora. So another level of interpretation is coming on to the Gospel, using a set of terms to try to describe the initial experience that are foreign to that experience. And certainly by the second and third centuries, from the neo-Platonic period onward, a whole new philosophical and epistemological layer is going to be added on to the Christian *kerygma*, trying to convey the mystical heart of the experience to a whole new generation of thinkers. In the end Greek philosophical language came to be so wedded to Christian theology—just like Roman law! —that we tend to think of it as almost canonical, inspired at the same level of authority as Scripture itself. But many scholars are quick and eager to point out that it is not, and not essential to the inner meaning of the Gospel and the experience of adoption, filiation, union, and divinization that Jesus inspires and offers.

What teachers such as Swāmī Abhishiktānanda asked was, what if Christianity could be interpreted and passed on using the language of the Vedānta (Indian philosophy, based on the Upanishads), the language of Mahāyāna Buddhism, or the language of Taoism or Confucian philosophy? And, if not then, why not now? Is it possible to take our experience of the

3. Stuart, *Swāmī Abhishiktānanda*, 349.

Gospel and our tradition, and try to articulate it using other philosophical or mystical language? This may perhaps be a primary contributing factor to the failure of evangelization efforts in Asia. We have used a philosophical language that in many cases makes little sense to the Asian mind. We have so often tried to pass on Greek terms and Roman culture (e.g., the Roman Rite of the Mass and Gregorian chant) instead of allowing the seed of the *kerygma* to take root in the soil of native philosophical and cultural, iconographic and poetic genius, acknowledging that the spark of the Divine and the inspiration of the Holy Spirit has been at work in other traditions as well. Swāmī Abhishiktānanda and Bede thought this was especially true in India, where Christianity failed to express the *kerygma* of Christianity in words and ideas capable of resonating with India's inmost depths. (Perhaps underlying this was a suspicion that many Christians themselves had not had the deep level of experience that the sages and rishis of India had had.)

In my own interreligious encounters I have often distinguished three different levels of inter-religious study, dialogue, and immersion: philosophical, practical, and devotional. As for the first, philosophical, the Catholic Church, beginning at least with *Nostra aetate*, the document on relations with Non-Christians of Vatican II, encouraged Catholics to be involved at this level. Most people forget that Christianity didn't have its own philosophy and so borrowed a "pagan" philosophy, from Greece, in order to articulate itself. Justin Martyr's famous defense of this was his idea of *semina verbi*, the "seeds of the Word" that were scattered everywhere, particularly for him in the Greek philosophers.

However, we have come to recognize those seeds of the Word in other places as well, as Pope John Paul II wrote in his letter *Fides et Ratio*:

> In preaching the Gospel, Christianity first encountered Greek philosophy; but this does not mean at all that other approaches are precluded. Today, as the Gospel gradually comes into contact with cultural worlds that once lay beyond Christian influence, there are new tasks of inculturation, which mean that our generation faces problems not unlike those faced by the Church in the first centuries.
>
> My thoughts turn immediately to the lands of the East, so rich in religious and philosophical traditions of great antiquity ... Among these lands, India has a special place. A great spiritual impulse leads Indian thought to seek an experience which would liberate the spirit from the shackles of time and space and would therefore acquire absolute value. The dynamic of this quest for liberation provides the context for great metaphysical systems.

> In India particularly, it is the duty of Christians now to draw from this rich heritage the elements compatible with their faith, in order to enrich Christian thought . . .[4]

The duty! (We Camaldolese Benedictines, by the way, have a special mandate from Pope John Paul II to involve ourselves in interreligious dialogue. It's part of our charism.) Hence, again, why we dearly cherish the legacy of Swāmī Abhishiktānanda.

Yoga is based on Sāmkhya philosophy, for instance, which is one of the six classical *dharshanas* (philosophies) of India, and it is actually *nontheistic*. There is no mention of any deities at all. And classical Yoga philosophy itself is only mildly theistic. The only name used for the Divine in the Yoga Sūtras of Patanjali is *Īshvara*, which means something like "Lord," and is a word that is used in Christian prayers in the vernacular as well. Part of the work those of us involved in interreligious dialogue do is to try to find out what of Sāmkhya and classical Yoga philosophy is "compatible with our faith." This is the genius of many of Swāmī Abhishiktānanda's writings; particularly again I point to his essay on *sannyāsa* (*The Further Shore*) and even more his book *Saccidānanda*, a book steeped in philosophy and comparative theology, written rather late in his life.

A second level is practical. In regards to Yoga, for instance, this entails the actual physical exercises of stretching and breathing, as well as the various methods of concentration in preparation for meditation. There was a "Letter to the Bishops of the Catholic Church on Some Aspects of Christian Meditation," issued by the Congregation for the Doctrine of the Faith in 1989, which we have good reason to believe came pretty much from the pen of Pope Emeritus Benedict himself when he was the head of that congregation. This is from Chapter V on "Questions of Method":

> The majority of the great religions that have sought union with God in prayer have also pointed out ways to achieve it. Just as "the Catholic church rejects nothing of what is true and holy in these religions," neither should these ways be rejected out of hand simply because they are not Christian. On the contrary, one can take from them what is useful so long as the Christian conception of prayer, its logic and requirements are never obscured. It is within the context of all of this that these bits and pieces should be taken up and expressed anew.[5]

---

4. John Paul II, *Fides et Ratio*, §72.
5. Congregation for the Doctrine of the Faith, "Letter," §16.

Foreword

I actually have a copy of the news article from 2005 when the same Pope Benedict gave permission for Yoga to be taught in the seminaries of India. So many of us have obviously found great health benefits, both physically and mentally, from Yoga. My own experience of religious life is that so many of our priests and religious here in the US are overweight and/or depressed, and take solace in alcohol or various forms of "self medication." It's no wonder that so many people look at folks from other traditions who are healthy and happy and wonder what they have got that we don't. And we *should* have it, because Christianity is supposedly the most incarnate of all the religious traditions. I no longer wonder if there is something "useful" we could actually learn; I am convinced of it.

As for the last, the devotional path (what is referred to in India as the *bhakti mārga*), there are obviously people who worship the deities of Hinduism. I do not and never encourage it; in fact I discourage Christians from it. Even when I visit India, I do not take part in temple services and *pūjas*. Then I would be in danger of idolatry. Yet when dealing with these poems of Swāmī Abhishiktānanda, we are certainly at the borderline of his own *bhakti*. We are also back once again to experience and language —how first of all to understand it, and then how to express this experience, let alone be transformed by it. Or perhaps we could start with the transformation itself! How do we understand and express it? Again I ask, how many songs have been written about the experience of falling in love, and yet do any of them ever fully capture it?

Swāmī Abhishiktānanda's poetry comes from this *bhakti* element in his spiritual life. If he wondered if Christians would perhaps "become angry, / crying, 'Sacrilege!' / when they hear that India's Sages and Rishis / here are heard and venerated / as Job and Melchizedek were" (as you shall read below), how much more so when they hear of him singing in praise of Shiva. And what about this concept of the *Purusha*?

One of the elements that Swāmī Abhishiktānanda and his peers (e.g., Bede Griffiths, Raimon Panikkar) open up for us is what is known as the apophatic dimension of spirituality in general and of Christianity in particular, that is, the recognition that the Divine is *anāmarūpa*—beyond name and form. This is sometimes referred to as the *via negativa*, the negative way. As Pope Benedict describes it, the characteristic feature of the apophatic way "is the conviction that it is impossible to say who God is, that only indirect things can be said about him; that God can only be spoken of with the 'not,' and that it is only possible to reach him by entering into this indirect experience of 'not.'"[6] In Christianity an apophatic strain traces all the way back to Gregory of Nyssa and Pseudo-Dionysius (about whom Benedict was writing the above words), *The Cloud of Unknowing*, Meister Eckhart, and especially John of the Cross, the latter of whom Swāmī Abhishiktānanda quoted often. Swāmī Abhishiktānanda wrote fervently about this mystical awareness beyond name and form, this awareness that gave him a sense of ever increasing internal peace.

One might be tempted to think, however, that this experience of the Divine beyond name and form is so iconoclastic as to be impersonal, as if God were just a nameless force of some sort, or solely the Ground of Being (Brahman) and/or the Ground of Consciousness (ātman). There is a famous story told by John Cassian in his *Conferences* about an "old man" of the desert whom Abba Paphnutius was able to convince that God was beyond all anthropomorphic images, that he could not "undergo anything typical of human experience and likeness" that could be observed "by the eye nor by the mind." But later they met that same old man breaking into the "bitterest, most abundant tears and sobs. He threw himself on the ground and with the mightiest howl he cried out: 'Ah the misfortune! They've taken my God away from me. I have no one to hold on to, and I don't know whom to adore or to address.'"[7] The opposite was true for Swāmī Abhishiktānanda: the encounter with this Ground *anāmarūpa* (beyond all name and form) sparked in him a new strain of devotion, of *bhakti*.

As an example of this strain of Swāmī Abhishiktānanda's experience and expression, note how many times "Shiva" appears in his writings. A cursory understanding might accuse this Catholic monk of idolatry, worshipping another god besides the Judeo-Christian one. Indeed, at the level of popular devotion Shiva is worshipped as one of the *trimūrti*—the trinity of Hindu gods along with Brahmā and Vishnu—represented as a yogi wearing a tiger skin holding a trident with snakes coiled around his neck and arms. But a deeper understanding of Shiva is that this is simply a name for the all-pervasive supreme reality who manifests in functions, qualities, and principles but that/who is beyond all name and form. Here, for example, are the first and last verses of the famous hymn of Shiva attributed to Ādi Shankara, the great eighth-century sage of Advaita Vedānta:

6. Benedict XVI, General Audience.
7. Cassian, *Conferences*, XIII.3.

> I am not mind, intellect, ego and the memory.
> I am not the sense organs.
> I am not the five elements.
> I am Shiva in the form of bliss consciousness.
> I am formless and devoid of all dualities.
> I exist everywhere and pervade all senses.
> Always I am the same,
> I am neither free nor bonded.
> I am Shiva in the form of bliss consciousness.[8]

And yet, as you will witness in his poetry, Swāmī Abhishiktānanda shows himself to be a devotee—a *bhakta* of this Ground of Being who is formless and devoid of all dualities, and a lover of this fathomless abyss of the godhead. There is a beautiful compound word in Sanskrit that describes Swāmī Abhishiktānanda well—*bhakti-rūpāpanna-jnāna*: not just love of God but knowledge that has become devotion. One way to see Swāmī Abhishiktānanda's path is that he entered into this experience of "not" and came out of it a lover of God in a whole new way.

Again you will read below a sentence our poet wrote in his diary that seems to capture his conviction as well as the energy behind his quest to reconcile his Christianity with this experience of the spiritual genius of India: "The experience of the Upanishads is true, *I know it!*"[9] And then he immediately quotes this famous "hymn" from the Shvetāshvatara Upanishad.

> *Vedāham etam purusham mahāntam*
> *ādityavarnam tamasah parastāt*
> *tameva viditvā ati mrityum eti*
> *nānya panthā vidyate'yanāya.*

> I know the Great Person [*Purusha*]
> of the color of the sun beyond darkness.
> Only by knowing that one do we overcome death.
> There is no other way to go.

Perhaps the main significance of this hymn is that it is part of the *sannyāsa dīkshā*, the initiation into the life of renunciation. As Swāmī Abhishiktānanda describes it in *The Further Shore*:

---

8. Ādi Shankara, *Ātmashatkam*. Foreword author's personal file.
9. Swāmī Abhishiktānanda, *Ascent to the Depth of the Heart*, 348–49.

Foreword

The new sannyāsi plunges into the water. Then the guru raises him like the Purusha of the Aitareyopanishad:

Arise, O Man! Arise, wake up, you who have received the boons; keep awake!

Both of them then face the rising sun and sing the song to the [Purusha] from the Uttara-Nārāyana:

I know him, that supreme Purusha, sun-coloured, beyond all darkness; only in knowing him one overcomes death; no other way exists.[10]

As I understand it there are multiple uses of the term *purusha*. At a mundane level, it can refer to an individual, akin to our English word "man," the non-inclusive word for human beings. (In Hindi, closely related to Sanskrit, indeed it is the word specifically for the male.) As Sāmkhya philosophy and classical Yoga use the term, *purusha* is the soul, the Self, pure consciousness, and the only source of consciousness. But this *purusha* is pure and distant, beyond subject and object. The term *purusha* can also, as we see in this hymn, designate the Cosmic Person, the Great Person, the original Self from which all else comes.

The Upanishads, which Swāmī Abhishiktānanda loved so much, are known for little mention of the deities, nor of sacrifice and rituals. They concern themselves mainly with the journey to the cave of the heart, where the Ground of Consciousness (ātman) realizes its identity with the Ground of Being (Brahman). Yet the notion of the Purusha as a personal god is not entirely missing from the Upanishads either. The Upanishads begin with Brahman, the mystery of being; then they come to the realization that this mystery of being is not different from ātman, the inner Self, and that the human self is one with the Supreme Self, the Being of the whole creation. But then, as thought develops further in the Upanishads, this ātman, this Brahman, comes to be seen as *Purusha*, who is not, however, just an impersonal ground of being nor an impersonal ground of consciousness, pure and distant, beyond subject and object, but *Purusha* as Person again, even an object of devotion.

There are already hints of this personal god even in early Upanishads, in the Brihadāranyaka and the Īsha, for example. But this strain is more fully developed in the Shvetāshvatara Upanishad, which is a rather late one. In chapter 1:7–9, we hear of the triad, the perishable, the imperishable, and

---

10. Swāmī Abhishiktānanda, *The Further Shore*, 54.

that which is beyond the two.[11] This third aspect, beyond perishable and imperishable, beyond that which is immanent in nature and consciousness, beyond the impersonal ground of being and ground of consciousness, is the *Purusha*, to whom Swāmī Abhishiktānanda reveals his devotion in that *sannyāsa* hymn from the same Shvetāshvatara Upanishad: "I know that Great Person of the color of the sun beyond darkness. Only by knowing that one do we overcome death."

In his spiritual diary Swāmī Abhishiktānanda writes, "God is invisible, non-manifested, *a-vyakta*. This God is the Father, the Source, the First [*Prathama*]."[12] In another place Swāmī Abhishiktānanda says of this passage that Christ himself is "the *Purusha* who looks on, while the 'other' *purusha* enjoys the world and lives in anxiety."[13] From a Christian standpoint, it is not that he has forsaken the Trinity nor the "persons" (whatever that word may mean!) in the Trinity, but he has instead found a new way to express his experience of them and It (the Trinity), with a new language and even a new ardor.

This is vitally important in our day and age when so many have grown jaded about and tired of the ponderous, limited, and exclusive language that often seems to be forced upon us. (See for example the latest English translation of the Roman Missal, slavishly faithful to the Latin in spite of the sometimes dubious theology that underlies the prayers themselves!) Someone like our pioneering wandering French poet strikes an attractive

---

11.
In song it has been called the supreme *brahman*.
    In it are the triad, the good support and the imperishable.
Knowing it and merging into *brahman*,
    knowers of *brahman*, intent on it, are freed from the womb.

The powerful one bears the whole, united,
    Perishable and imperishable, manifest and unmanifest.
The self, powerless, is bound through its being an enjoyer.
    Once it knows the god, it is freed from all bonds.

There are two billy goats, knower and unknowing, powerful and powerless;
    One nanny goat, yoked to the enjoyer and the objects of enjoyment;
And the infinite self, possessing all forms, not an actor.
    When one finds the triad, this is *brahman*.

Roebuck, *The Upanishads*, 296.
12. Swāmī Abhishiktānanda, *Ascent to the Depth of the Heart*, 284.
13. Ibid.

figure, not only fearlessly delving into the depth experience but ecstatically expressing it—as well as writing it down and leaving us a permanent record.

In his audience discussing Dionysius the Areopagite, Benedict XVI goes on to say that a mystic such as Dionysius (and by extension the apophatic way itself) has a new relevance today. Just as in his own day Dionysius was a mediator between the spirit of Greek philosophy and the Gospel, today these mystics who can speak of God beyond name and form can function as great mediators in the modern dialogue between Christianity and the mystical theologies of Asia, because there is "a similarity . . . between the thought of the Areopagite and that of Asian religions."[14] And here Pope Benedict, who at first glance might seem an odd bedfellow for our intrepid Breton, says something that Swāmī Abhishiktānanda could hardly disagree with. We can begin to understand "that dialogue does not accept superficiality" because

> it is precisely when one enters into the depths of the encounter with Christ that an ample space for dialogue also opens. When one encounters the light of truth, one realizes that it is a light for everyone; polemics disappear and it is possible to understand one another, or at least to speak to one another, to come closer. . . . And in the end, he tells us: take the path of experience, the humble experience of faith, every day.[15]

Today, as the Gospel has come into new kinds of contact with cultural worlds that once lay beyond Christian influence, Swāmī Abhishiktānanda aids us in the new tasks of inculturation and helps our generation face problems not unlike those faced by the Church in the first centuries. By entering into this experience of "not," by entering into the depths of encounter with Christ, Swāmī Abhishiktānanda, our modern Dionysius, serves as a mediator in our ongoing dialogue with the mystical theology of Asia in general and with the spiritual genius of India in particular. He opens for us a new language for articulating the Christian religious experience as well as, and most importantly, an invitation into a new depth experience of Christianity.

Cyprian Consiglio, OSB Cam.
New Camaldoli Hermitage
Big Sur, CA

---

14. Benedict XVI, "General Audience."
15. Ibid.

Preface and Acknowledgments

I ARRIVED AT OSAGE Monastery (a Benedictine monastery modeled on Hindu āshrams outside Sand Springs, Oklahoma) for the first time on the evening of St. Stephen's day of 2007. After the community's evening prayer and meditation, I passed by the small bookcase next to the front door of the main building that served as a bookshop. There I noted in addition to a number of larger volumes by Fr. Bede Griffiths a set of slimmer volumes by someone named "Swāmī Abhishiktānanda." By the style of their binding and the feel of their paper I knew clearly they had been printed in India, and most had geometric designs on their covers. I was immediately intrigued, sat down on the floor next to the shelves, and flipped a book open. After reading a paragraph or two of *In Spirit and Truth*, I put enough money to buy three books into the small tin on the bottom shelf and scurried silently back to my cabin in the woods.

That evening, I found something articulated that I had struggled to articulate for a number of years. Swāmī Abhishiktānanda's words sang with such candor and passion of a tremendous vision of who we humans are, what the world is, and how the Trinity informs it all. His Vedantic perspective on the Christian mystical and contemplative life floored me, causing a slow smile to spread across my face again and again in the dim light of the small cabin below the Forest's—the affectionate name for Osage—dark canopy. Since that time, Swāmījī has been a regular teacher, inspiration, and challenge to me through his writings, and it brings me great joy to present to the world his collected poems for the first time in this English translation.

This project was very much a labor of love, and there are a number of people dear to me whom I wish to thank. First and foremost, I would like to thank Swāmī Abhishiktānanda himself—for helping me find a sense of home in the great, teeming, complex reality of human history, religion, and culture.

Preface and Acknowledgments

My deep and filial gratitude also go to Sr. Pascaline Coff, Sr. Sarah Schwartzberg, and all the Benedictine Sisters of Perpetual Adoration for their witness, instruction, and friendship, and most especially for making Osage Monastery (now Osage Forest of Peace) a place of silence and peace amidst an often noisy and distracted world.

This project would not have been possible without the guidance and warmth of Swāmī Ātmānanda Udāsīn of Swāmī Ajātānanda Āshram in Rishikesh, India, director of the Abhishiktānanda Centre for Interreligious Dialogue, who invited me to take up this translation project and gave me permission to publish this material. He also guided me throughout amidst his own busy schedule and offered suggestions and corrections on the manuscript. Who would have thought when I emailed the Centre out of the blue in early 2015 that we would bring Swāmījī's poems to the world in three years' time!

My thanks likewise go to Fr. Cyprian Consiglio, Prior of New Camaldoli Hermitage in Big Sur, California, for his promotion of interreligious dialogue and the universal call to contemplation through his music, writing, retreats, and shepherding of the monks and oblates at New Camaldoli, and for taking the time to contribute the Foreword to this book—especially as he and his monks were dealing with the logistical fallout from landslides that had covered their access roads on the coast outside Big Sur when he composed it!

In a similar vein, I thank and acknowledge the support of Fr. William Skudlarek, Benedictine of St. John's Abbey in Collegeville, Minnesota, for his assistance throughout this project, his own contributions to promoting Swāmī Abhishiktānanda's teaching and legacy, and his work with Monastic Interreligious Dialogue, which carries on in an official capacity the valuable work begun by Swāmī Abhishiktānanda and others.

My appreciation also extends to everyone at the āshram of Shrī Ramana Maharshi in Tamil Nadu, India, especially Vaidyanathan, whose patience with my queries was impressive and constant. Swāmījī's first real glimpse of India and the spiritual riches she had to offer a Breton Christian monk, as well as the Church at large, occurred in the caves of Arunāchala and the āshram's environs, and their blessing on this work that presents Swāmījī's renderings of Shrī Ramana's own poems is both an honor and humbling.

The only other person I know of who had taken on the task of studying and making available Swāmī Abhishiktānanda's poetry was the late Judson Trapnell. Though I never met Dr. Trapnell, I have read and respect his work and wish the world could have seen what he was going to make

Preface and Acknowledgments

of the corpus I present below. However, Dr. Ted Ulrich of the University of St. Thomas in Minnesota very kindly and generously made available to me Dr. Trapnell's archival work and beginning plans for a study of these poems. Access to these preliminary materials helped me clarify the scope and direction of this project at its beginning, and I am tremendously grateful to Dr. Trapnell for the clearly heart-felt work he put into the project and to Dr. Ulrich for sharing the materials with me. I hope this volume is at least in part a fulfillment of Dr. Trapnell's vision.

Several of my friends and colleagues helped me wade through this material, and I appreciate their expertise, patience, and camaraderie—Andrew Klein helped me get started; Emily Ransom looked over the manuscript, making suggestions, and both she and Karl Persson let me talk their ears off about Swāmījī and his spiritual teaching (even when they didn't realize it); Liza Strakhov supported my French when I saw it faltering. Throughout the various stages of this project, Kerry Olivetti, Joan Sommer, and the Interlibrary Loan staff—Vicki Meinecke, John Lunt, and Katie Eigner—at Marquette University's Raynor Library searched out a number of obscure, out-of-print, and/or foreign-language volumes for me with unrelenting effort. To all of you: thank you!

Amidst all of this help and support, any lingering errors remain my own.

And finally, profound thanks to my parents, who early on encouraged my curiosity about other cultures and the world's religions—I still recall vividly the day we visited Avol's Books just off State Street in Madison, Wisconsin when I was no more than fifteen and they encouraged me to buy a small translation of the *Bhagavad Gītā* I had found down low on a set of black lacquered shelves; my brother, Paul, who, among other contributions, introduced me to Buddhist meditation techniques up in his bedroom when I was twelve; and my wife, Mamie, who has come on a very meandering and arcane road with me and has yet to let her enthusiasm, wonder, or love flag.

Jacob Riyeff
Marquette University
Milwaukee, WI

Introduction

AT THE HEART OF western Christian mysticism lies the experience of Trinitarian life—the Christian's participation in the mutual being of the Father and the Son in the communion of the Spirit. At the heart of Advaita Vedānta (a prominent school of Hindu religious thought and culture) lies the non-dual experience of the self as the Self, of the individual as ultimately identical with the transcendent principle of all reality—*aham brahmāsmi* (I am Brahman) as the Brihadāranyaka Upanishad (1.4.10) says; *tat tvam asi* (you are that) as the Chāndogya Upanishad (6.8.6) says.[1] Though these experiences both penetrate to profound questions about ultimate human realities, they of course were experienced initially and have developed within distinct religious communities and cultures over centuries and millennia. The French Benedictine monk, Dom Henri Le Saux (1910-1973)—later known as Swāmī Abhishiktānanda—strove to engage both these traditions in his life as a Christian monk and priest and as a *sannyāsī* (Hindu renunciate) throughout the two-and-a-half decades that he spent in India.

While Swāmī Abhishiktānanda has been understood as a prophet of interreligious dialogue, an inspiring figure for understanding at the deepest levels of who we are as human beings, and a realized guide on the spiritual and mystic paths, he is also often seen as a person of great contradiction. He himself certainly felt this contradiction and expressed the dual identity he saw within himself fervently: "an interior agony which is both dislocating and fulfilling."[2] And yet, one wonders if in today's post-conciliar Church and postmodern, globalized world Swāmī Abhishiktānanda would have experienced the same turmoil in his "double-path." Indeed, Raimon Panikkar (1918–2010), a fellow Catholic priest, prolific proponent of interreligious

1. For specialized terminology and for words in languages other than English, see the Glossary at the end of this volume.

2. Quoted in Baumer-Despeigne, "The Spiritual Way of Henri Le Saux," 20–21.

dialogue, and one of Swāmī Abhishiktānanda's closest friends, claims in a posthumous "letter" written to the Swāmī as the foreword to Shirley du Boulay's biography of the monk that such "double belonging" simply was and is not as problematic as Swāmī Abhishiktānanda envisioned it.

> You were not aware of how much you remained (like most Westerners) a disciple of Parmenides: reality could not be contradictory. And here was the source of your anguish at finding yourself to be at the same time Christian and Hindu, monotheist and *advaitin*. For me this was no problem at all, not only because I see no contradiction but also because I do not identify reality with rationality. The real is not obliged to obey Parmenides, and we do not fall into irrationality if we are aware of it. I think that the issue of "double belonging" . . . is still a false problem. . . . Your anguish came out of a dialectical thinking. Your greatness was that you overcame dialectical thinking not by another way of thinking but through painful and excruciating experience. That experience was enormously fruitful. You remained loyal to two dialectically opposed worldviews. For this, we are grateful to you.[3]

Drawing from his journals and letters, as well as accounts from those who knew him best, Swāmī Abhishiktānanda appears to have realized and embraced the reconciliation of this seeming contradiction in the last years of his life. Yet Panikkar is right to point out how important Swāmī Abhishiktānanda's own perception of his call as a contradiction was. For from a desire to understand, to analyze, but also to move beyond this existential and dialectical dilemma, Swāmī Abhishiktānanda gave the world a number of books that attest to his spiritual and profound human insights into the nature of being, the divine, the human, and the non-duality of the great mystery of the "I AM."

The same creative tension but less of the underlying anxiety, the same acute reflections on living an interreligious life, the same penetrating insight into the intimate depths of both the Upanishadic, Advaitic and Christian experience are all on full display in the poems that comprise this book. These poems were composed in French (with one exception) over the course of two decades and are rarely discussed in studies of Swāmī Abhishiktānanda's life and thought. This book invites the casual reader, the Christian, the Hindu, the sympathetic practitioner of other faiths and none, the lover of poetry, the scholar of poetry, the religious studies specialist, the

---

3. Panikkar, "Foreword," xiii.

INTRODUCTION

theologian, the monk to read these poems and reflect upon their message(s) and form(s) as Swāmī Abhishiktānanda offers his readers a vivid account of a life lived in the simultaneously terrible and beautiful light of the Trinitarian and Advaitic experiences.

Swāmī Abhishiktānanda's Life

As there are two full biographies of Swāmī Abhishiktānanda and shorter biographical treatments in several other works, I will give only a brief sketch of his life here.[4] Henri Le Saux was born to Alfred and Louise (Sonnefraüd) Le Saux on August 30, 1910 in Saint Briac, Brittany. The family was devoutly Catholic, and he entered the major seminary at Rennes at sixteen. After the death of a friend who had desired to become a Benedictine, Le Saux felt that he had "inherited" this vocation and entered the Abbey of Sainte-Anne of Kergonan in 1929. He made his solemn monastic vows on May 9, 1935 and was ordained (taking the additional name, Briac) on December 21 of that year. After several years of quiet monastic life, Le Saux was called up in 1939 for military service during the Second World War—being caught and escaping back to his monastery in July of 1940. After his work as librarian and soldier, he became the monastery's master of ceremonies, for which he was well remembered among the brothers.

Though the precise origins of the Indian connection remain unknown, a letter survives in which Le Saux recounts that his great desire to travel to India and establish the Christian contemplative life there in an inculturated form began to develop as early as 1934.[5] After years of searching for a "home" on the subcontinent, a French priest named Jules Monchanin, who had arrived in India in 1939 and had similar hopes of establishing the contemplative life in India, was presented with Le Saux's letter, and plans for a joint venture began. In particular, Le Saux was interested in the prospect of a mutual rethinking of Christian dogma through Hindu categories and concepts and of Hindu thought through Christian categories and concepts. All this was, of course, prophetic of what would come later in the Second Vatican Council (1962–65); at the time it was practically unheard of. He

---

4. Most of the details presented here are taken from du Boulay, *The Cave of the Heart*. The other major biography is Stuart, *Swāmī Abhishiktānanda*.

5. Found in Swāmī Abhishiktānanda's letter to Jules Monchanin dated August 18, 1947, *The Eyes of Light*, 9.

arrived in India August 15, 1948 and acclimated for a time under Monchanin's guidance.

During this time of travel and discovery, Monchanin took Le Saux to the āshram of Shrī Ramana Maharshi (1879–1950) in Tiruvannamalai, Tamil Nadu. Shrī Ramana was widely recognized as a sage of the highest order, a liberated being having realized the Self. He taught Advaita Vedānta, the non-dual (*advaita* being a Sanskrit word for nonduality—*a-* "not" and *dvaita* "duality") intuition found in the Upanishads that the innermost self of the individual, the Self, is in truth "not-two" with the Absolute (Brahman). This insight, once experienced by Le Saux in response to Shrī Ramana's presence, would remain a guiding light for the rest of his life. By the time Le Saux arrived in India, Shrī Ramana's āshram had developed into a finely tuned institution built around providing masses of devotees and pilgrims with the holy man's *darshana*. This state of affairs initially put Le Saux off, yet in short order he began to see Shrī Ramana as an embodiment of India's religious culture and discerned in him the unique Sage of the eternal India, and these insights penetrated into his own spiritual depths. The French Benedictine was permanently changed by the unassuming sage of Arunāchala—the holy mountain Shrī Ramana had inhabited as a younger man and at which Shrī Ramana's āshram had grown up around him.

Two years after Shrī Ramana's death in 1950, Le Saux lived in a cave hermitage at Arunāchala in silence and meditation, which he describes in his book *The Secret of Arunāchala*. By this time he wore the *kāvi* robes of a Hindu *sannyāsī* consistently and had taken the name "Swāmī Abhishikteshvarānanda" ("he whose bliss is the Anointed Lord"), which was further shortened to "Abhishiktānanda." This period was a formative one for Swāmī Abhishiktānanda, one in which he began to experience the Advaitic intuition of non-duality, which he understood "as the equivalent of the intuition of Moses in Exodus and of Jesus: *I am*."[6] It is also particularly important for this book, since much of the material in the first two sections presented here were first drafted during Swāmī Abhishiktānanda's time at Arunāchala. He describes the first poem in this book, "Arunāchala," as being "sung to me by Arunāchala one night before I went to sleep, and I relit my lamp several times to catch it. Perhaps it will convey some of the spell cast upon me by Arunāchala."[7]

---

6. Panikkar, "Introduction," xiv.
7. Stuart, *Swāmī Abhishiktānanda*, 76 n. 31.

Introduction

Before this, on the feast of St. Benedict, March 21, 1950, Monchanin and Swāmī Abhishiktānanda inaugurated Saccidānanda ("being, consciousness, bliss"—the attributes of the ultimate, unchanging reality in Vedānta) Āshram at a site called Shāntivanam ("forest of peace") in Tamil Nadu. It was to be a Benedictine āshram, a place of solitude, silence, and contemplation, a place where Christians and Hindus, where Christianity and Hinduism, could come together to inform one another. Notably, both Christian hermits saw the venture as preeminently one of inculturation of Indian Christianity based on a "fulfillment theology," one that saw Christianity as the superior religion toward which other religions must tend and find their divine fulfillment. Swāmī Abhishiktānanda would distance himself from this perspective as he came to realize the Truth of Advaita. He later became an emblematic figure of the monastic interreligious dialogue.[8]

Swāmī Abhishiktānanda lived at Shāntivanam until 1968, but this period saw his burgeoning longing to immerse himself in Advaita, to delve deeper into the experience of his Hindu brothers and sisters, especially that of Shrī Ramana Maharshi and his disciples at Arunāchala. The daily running of the ashram was often a strain for him, though in a different way from the strain of his increasingly tense spiritual life. At this time too, he had sent to the censor in Paris a copy of his first articulation of emerging ideas based in Advaitic experience, a book he called *Guhāntara*, which included poems later incorporated into the typescripts that form the basis of the present volume. The book was utterly rejected by the censor in 1954 and has yet to find publication, though most of its prose content has been published in two posthumous volumes.[9]

In 1955, Swāmī Abhishiktānanda was informed of Shrī Gnānānanda Giri, a sage living in Tirukoyilūr, not far from Arunāchala. In this man Swāmī Abhishiktānanda discovered the true nature of the guru-disciple relationship, Shrī Gnānānanda accepting the Christian *sannyāsī* as his disciple and requesting that he come for a retreat at the former's āshram to engage in silent *dhyāna* beyond form and so awaken to the Self. Through his experiences in Shrī Gnānānanda's ashram and in the town's temple, Swāmī Abhishiktānanda came to embrace the outer manifestations of Hindu religious culture much more readily and openly than he had in the past.

---

8. For an account of how monastic interreligious dialogue drifted from its origins in explicit missionary work toward a model of dialogue that seeks to accept monastics from other religions as they are, see Blée, *The Third Desert*.

9. Swāmī Abhishiktānanda, *Initiation à la spiritualité des Upanishads*; Swāmī Abhishiktānanda, *Intériorité et révélation*.

Towards the end of 1956, in accordance with Shrī Gnānānanda's counsel, Swāmī Abhishiktānanda spent thirty-two days in silent retreat at a Mauna Mandir (Temple of Silence) in Kumbakonam. It is perhaps here that he had the most intense experience of solitude and silence, living in the tradition not only of his Hindu teachers, but also of St. Benedict, of whom St. Gregory had written, "Then he returned to the solitary place he delighted in and dwelt alone, in the presence of the celestial Witness, with himself."[10]

After leaving Kumbakonam, Swāmī Abhishiktānanda travelled extensively, seeing new places, visiting friends, preaching, and keeping some distance between himself and Shāntivanam, from which he was planning to depart for good. However, Fr. Monchanin fell ill and died soon after, and Swāmī Abhishiktānanda felt obliged to take over guidance of Shāntivanam, remaining there, intermittently, until 1968. While he remained conflicted about the nature of the āshram and his role there, he used his years of leadership to advance more communal and regular meetings of Christians interested in dialogue with Hinduism, and many of his formal contributions to Hindu-Christian dialogue come from this period. He received Indian citizenship in 1960, published some of his most well-known volumes throughout the mid-sixties, and expanded his social circle appreciably among Catholic, Anglican, and Hindu friends. His ideas and writing began to be more warmly accepted among larger and broader audiences. During this time he also began planning how to settle in the one place in his travels that consistently called him—beside the holy river Ganges in the Himalayas. Panikkar purchased some land for Swāmī Abhishiktānanda in 1961, on the banks of the Ganges at Gyansū (Uttarkāshī), and a *kutiyā* (hermitage) was built for him later that year. Yet Swāmī Abhishiktānanda did not move there permanently right away, instead splitting his time between the north and the south for several years. Finally, in 1968, he decided to leave Shāntivanam in the hands of the English Benedictine Bede Griffiths, who came from Kurisumala Āshram in Kerala, a community established by the Belgian Cistercian Francis Mahieu Acharya in 1958 (founded at Tiruvalla

---

10. "*Tunc ad locum dilectae solitudinis rediit, et solus in superni spectatoris oculis habitauit se cum*"; Gregory the Great, *Dialogi*, II.3. Swāmī Abhishiktānanda was keenly influenced by this description of the solitude of monastic life in the Benedictine model ("*se cum*," "with himself"), citing it three times in his spiritual diary—twice while staying in the caves at Arunāchala and once while reflecting on his retreat at the Mauna Mandir—and equating it to the Sanskrit term *ātmanishtha* (*Ascent to the Depth of the Heart*, 51, 66, and 184).

in 1956).[11] The last stage of his life, as a hermit in the north of India amidst the Himalayas on the banks of the Ganges, had begun.

Settling in his one-room hut in Gyansū in 1968, he embraced the eremitic life of silence, study, and absorption with increased dedication. He had visitors and traveled as before but devoted more time to stability and solitude. After only a few years, Swāmī Abhishiktānanda finally became a guru in his own right, having few disciples from among several people who had approached him for instruction throughout the late sixties and early seventies: a seminarian from Bourg named Marc Chaduc (b. 1944), who arrived in India in 1971, and Sr. Thérèse de Jésus, a Carmelite novice-mistress at Lisieux who arrived in India in 1965.

In Marc in particular, it became quite clear that Swāmī Abhishiktānanda finally found a perfect disciple for whom he became a guru. The intensity of the two men's relationship was sudden and mutual, and they shared remarkable experiences of awakening together at Phulchatti Āshram and Shivānanda Āshram in northern India. At this time and directly related to these experiences with his disciple, Swāmī Abhishiktānanda wrote fervently of the mystical awareness beyond name and form and the concomitant peace that increasingly held sway in his life. Swāmī Abhishiktānanda experienced great fulfillment in his guru-disciple relationship with Marc. On June 30, 1973, Swāmī Abhishiktānanda and Swāmī Chidānanda (1916-2008), a living realized sage and the *acharya* of Shivānanda Āshram, initiated Marc into the highest *sannyāsa*, the *vidvat sannyāsa*, in an "ecumenical" *dīkshā*—Swāmī Abhishiktānanda welcoming the new Swāmī Ajātānanda into Christian monastic life reaching back to the Desert Fathers and Mothers and Swāmī Chidānanda welcoming him into the Hindu tradition of renunciation, in the lineage of Ādi Shankara. It was to be one of the culminating moments in Swāmī Abhishiktānanda's life. Swāmī Ajātānanda left the *dīkshā* to wander as a *sannyāsī*. After several years of seclusion and wandering, Swāmī Ajātānanda disappeared from his *kutiyā* (hermitage) sometime in early 1977, and what happened to him has not come to light. In a strange coincidence, Sr. Thérèse de Jésus also disappeared from her hermitage in the Himalayas.

Throughout 1973, Swāmī Abhishiktānanda grew more reticent to participate in seminars and other formal forums, sensing that his teaching was no longer appropriate to such venues. As he began to look for a

---

11. For Francis Acharya and the history and mission of Kurisumala Āshram, see Mahieu-De Praetere, *Kurisumala* and Francis Acharya, *Cistercian Spirituality*.

new place to settle due to ailing health, Swāmī Abhishiktānanda met with Swāmī Ajātānanda one last time at a small Shiva temple at Ranagal (north of Rishikesh), where the two shared several days of intense inner and inter- experience. When Swāmī Abhishiktānanda went to Rishikesh on July 14 to find food for their retreat, he suffered a heart attack and was found on the sidewalk a while later by a member of Shivānanda Āshram. For the next several months he was taken care of by a *brahmachari* of Shivānanda Āshram, sent by Swāmī Chidānanda, then briefly by a community of Quakers at Rājpur, and finally by Mother Théophane at a nursing home run by the French Franciscan Sisters of St. Mary of the Angels at Indore. Though seriously weakened, Swāmī Abhishiktānanda experienced a deep spiritual awakening, as he described in his diary.

> The centre of the intuition that impressed itself upon me during those very first days [after July 14] was that the Awakening is independent of any situation whatever, of all the pairs of opposites [*dvandvas*], and first of all of the *dvandva* of life/death. . . .
>
> After some days there came to me, as if it were the marvelous solution to an equation: I have found the Grail. And that is what I keep saying and writing to anyone who can grasp the figure of speech. The quest for the Grail is basically nothing else than the quest for the Self. A single quest, that is the meaning of all the myths and symbols. It is yourself that you are seeking through everything. And in this quest you run about everywhere, whereas the Grail is here, close at hand, you only have to open your eyes. . . .
>
> In those weeks of grace I got the very clear impression that a "new lease" of life had been given me, something beyond the span allotted to me by "life," and that I have no right to misuse it. This grace of awakening—of returning to life—is not for my sake but for others. It was so clear: to announce the discovery of the Grail, to tell people: *Uttishta, purusha,* Arise, Purusha! (K[atha] U[panishad] 3.14), discover the Grail. Look, it is in the depth of yourself, it is the very "I" that you are saying every moment of your conscious life, even in the depth of your consciousness when you dream or sleep. A life from now on that is at the service of this Awakening.[12]

After several months of this awakened life, Swāmī Abhishiktānanda left the body in his *mahāprasthāna* (great journey) on December 7, 1973.

---

12. Swāmī Abhishiktānanda, *Ascent to the Depth of the Heart*, 385-86.

Perhaps the most fitting conclusion to this brief biographical sketch in a book of Swāmī Abhishiktānanda's poems is to note one final observation he made in a letter to his sister, Sr. Marie-Thérèse Le Saux. His comment pinpoints the resolution of a particularly representative paradox in Swāmī Abhishiktānanda's life: that of reality and symbol, experience and reflection.

> It is remarkable that you were moved to implore help for me at the very time when I was lying helpless on my sidewalk! Everything was so wonderful in those first two weeks. Later came the stripping away of all thought, meditation, contemplation. Now it is simply a matter of *being there* and being awake without feeling any of the poetry of the awakening.
>
> I shall be quite unable to write any poetry for you in return, '*ut jumentum*' . . . The joy often went with marvelous poetry; now there is the joy without any poetry, and that is only the more true.[13]

But for those of us not yet on "the other shore," there is still the chance of joy with "marvelous poetry."

Swāmī Abhishiktānanda's Importance for Interreligious Dialogue

In the decades since Swāmī Abhishiktānanda's death, interreligious dialogue has come to be a mainstay of Christian monastic life in the West, officially supported by the Catholic Church and monastic authorities. Among many other important statements, in the document *Nostra aetate* promulgated by the Second Vatican Council, the council fathers exhorted all the faithful "that through dialogue and collaboration with the followers of other religions, carried out with prudence and love and in witness to the Christian faith and life, they recognize, preserve, and promote the good things, spiritual and moral, as well as the socio-cultural values found among" their adherents.[14]

While *Nostra aetate* calls all Christians to encounter and dialogue, we find the heart of this movement of interreligious dialogue over the past half-century and more to be primarily a monastic phenomenon. Watershed meetings of monastics from various religions at Bangkok in 1968 and Bangalore in 1973 built on the goals of Aide à l'Implantation Monastique

---

13. Stuart, *Swāmī Abhishiktānanda*, 357. "*ut jumentum*": "like a beast," Ps 72:23.

14. Paul VI, "Declaration on the Relation of the Church to Non-Christian Religions," § 2.

(AIM; founded by the Benedictines in 1959) and lead to further meetings at Petersham, Massachusetts and Loppem, Belgium in 1977. At these later meetings, the constituent members of the current organization for monastic interreligious dialogue, Dialogue Interreligieux Monastique/ Monastic Interreligious Dialogue (DIMMID), were founded.[15] In 1996, the first Gethsemani Encounter occurred, drawing monastics and allies from various Catholic and Buddhist orders together at Thomas Merton's former abbey in Kentucky, including His Holiness the Fourteenth Dalai Lama. Three such encounters have been held since, sparking deep sharing between participants and also leading to interreligious publications. Swāmī Abhishiktānanda offers his reasoning for monastics' centrality to this cause in the Church in his last formal essay written before his death.

> It is therefore perfectly natural that monks of every dharma [used here to denote the entirety of a particular religion] should recognize each other as brothers across frontiers of their respective dharmas. This follows from that very transcendence of all signs to which all of them bear witness. . . . It is enough that they should thus recognize each other whenever they happen to meet, and in fact those who are genuine do infallibly respond to each other. Despite all differences in observance, language, and cultural background, they perceive in each other's eyes that depth which the One Spirit has opened in their own hearts. They sense the bliss, the light, the ineffable peace which emanate from it; and when they embrace each other, as they so often spontaneously do, it is a sign that they have felt and recognized their innate "non-duality," for in truth in the sphere of the *ajāta*, the unborn, there is no "otherness."[16]

For Swāmī Abhishiktānanda then, it is this common, "unquenchable desire for the Absolute" across the various religions that enables monastics and others of their spiritual inclination to recognize one another and dialogue, sharing insights as they retain their own religious commitments.

Even with this clear enthusiasm for such encounters, we do sense in Swāmī Abhishiktānanda's words quoted above a certain reticence about organized and programmatic dialogue such as has been built upon his example and that of other "fathers" of monastic interreligious dialogue

---

15. The history of modern monastic interreligious dialogue is described in Blée, *The Third Desert*.

16. Swāmī Abhishiktānanda, *The Further Shore*, 26-27.

Introduction

like Thomas Merton and Bede Griffiths.[17] While intermittently involved in various formal groups doing the collective work of interreligious dialogue, Swāmī Abhishiktānanda generally shied away from institutional ties and programs. His was a personal venture into the unknown spaces shared by the Hindu and Christian religions. He felt that a Christian could enter the Advaitic experience of Vedānta with faith retained on "the other side," and understood the Trinity as essentially non-dual (see appendix).

He saw in particular how the interaction of Christian and Hindu understandings of the Divine could clear away Christians' complacency and ossified adherence to formulas, spurring them on to a fresh encounter with their own understandings of the Trinity.

> Popular religion finds it quite natural to be satisfied with rites and formulas. "Let there be an agreement between us and God! We will offer him all the sacrifices that he has prescribed. But then let him leave us in peace. He may also give us a nice simple catechism and a well formulated theology, free from obscure ideas. We will gladly recite the Creeds and confess, for example, that there is only One God in three Persons, and that the Word was made flesh, died and rose again. But we hope he will limit his requirements to this, and will not expect these formulas to make any impression on our thinking or our lives!" Popular religion comforts and satisfies men; but only too often it empties out the essential restlessness implanted by God in the heart. On the other hand, the secret and irresistible attraction of the unknown poses questions which remain forever unanswered. He who thinks he understands, understands nothing but his own thought. There is no possible response except to "take off." Without dying there is no passage beyond death.
>
> From the depths of the soul, from the silence at the source of being, rises the fundamental question: "Who am I?" This very question is itself the revelation of Brahman.
>
> For this question reduces the spirit to silence, a silence which is itself Reality and Truth. This is the Silence from which the Word sprang forth in the bosom of the Father, as Ignatius of Antioch reminded the Magnesians. But this Word is uttered and heard at a level of the self which transcends phenomenal consciousness. It is not a word born of human thought or the human mind, but the very Word in which all things have their source, the Vedic OM, the primordial utterance. It is the Logos, the Word through whom all things were made, in whom, at the "dawn" of eternity (if one

---

17. Ibid., 33–34.

may so express it), the Father, the Source and Beginning, awoke to himself.[18]

Swāmī Abhishiktānanda adopts Hindu ways of relating to the most profound depths of the relationship between humanity and God to shake us awake—to place the irreducible demand of being, of non-duality, of participation in divine life immediately before his audience. Though we could read his pronouncements on the proclivities of popular religion as elitist, there is an urgency here that is dissatisfied with any religion demanding less than a genuine transformation of the practitioner that denounces hypocrisy and sloth wherever they are found rather than any "unwashed masses."[19] Swāmī Abhishiktānanda never sounds so much like the fiery monastic reformers of the Middle Ages as when he emphasized the importance of having the direct experience of the Divine Reality.

The precise nature of Swāmī Abhishiktānanda's theological thought in such interreligious assertions and explorations need not concern us here in their particulars. Suffice it to say that he understood his own religious odyssey as one wholly informed by Advaita, yet he retained his Christian faith until the end and regularly expressed his insights and experiences in terms other than those of strict Advaita Vedānta. Reading some of these poems, one might see reflected the Hindu tradition of *bhakti yoga*, a spiritual path trod by those called to love God with fervent devotion, like the famous Mirabai (ca. 1498–1557). While this is so, such love imagery is not foreign to the Advaita tradition Swāmī Abhishiktānanda drew upon. In fact, Shrī Ramana Maharshi, whose poems Swāmī Abhishiktānanda made "renderings" of in the 1950s and which are included here in section two, employed similar language from the tradition of love poetry in his own non-dual teaching.

While such questions are of great interest for understanding Swāmī Abhihiktānanda and for moving interreligious dialogue forward, these are in the end theological and philosophical questions. As such, the solutions to their intricacies need not prevent one interested in Swāmī Abhishiktānanda's poetry from encountering it on its own ground. In fact, Swāmī Abhishiktānanda's own insistence on the need *not* to get caught up in conceptual frameworks and definitions makes the immediacy and profligacy of his poems all the more important as a balancing element in

18. Swāmī Abhishiktānanda, *Hindu-Christian Meeting Point*, 56-57.
19. Swāmī Abhishiktānanda readily identified in his ideals and in his daily life with the poorest of India's poor, helping his neighbors with his meager means as well until his death.

INTRODUCTION

his larger corpus. In a way, the irreducibility of a poem to a paraphrase reflects the resistance of mystical experience to precise expression in words. Letting the poem *be* can prevent us from succumbing to the need to rationalize the immediate experience of the Divine, as mystics like Swāmī Abhishiktānanda encourage us to do across divisions of religion, culture, language, philosophy, nation, and time.

Swāmī Abhishiktānanda's Poems

Although Swāmī Abhishiktānanda is not known as a poet, he prepared two separate but overlapping collections of French poems for publication and inserted poetic passages into a number of his prose texts. These latter are present in his diary, letters, and prose essays and books. Throughout these pieces, Swāmī Abhishiktānanda consistently draws on two basic formal modes—two modes of writing "poetically"—neither of which utilizes a regular metrical form. In both poetic collections he prepared, we find on the one hand pieces rendered in free verse centered on the page, generally built around relatively short phrases and clauses and concrete images; on the other hand, we find free verse pieces rendered in longer and more elaborate lines, set on the left-hand margin, that deal more often with abstract ideas and nonetheless break regularly, usually around a line-and-a-half to two lines. The former style is found again in the poems composed in his letters, especially those written for Swāmī Ajātānanda. The latter form predominates in his journal and other prose writings.

Though Swāmī Abhishiktānanda does not utilize set poetic forms with regular meters, several formal features, like vivid and even shocking images, ardent anaphora, and syntactic parallelism, characterize his free verse. While certainly there is a degree of impressionistic judgment involved in this assessment—especially when determining the beginnings and endings of the poems found in Swāmī Abhishiktānanda's diary—anyone familiar with the Swāmī's fervent desire and the defining thought found in his prose works will note a related but different tone in his poetic works. Here there is an immediacy and a baldness (boldness!) of statement and observation he did not often allow himself. Here in the poems, Swāmī Abhishiktānanda lets his guard down more than he does in his prose, the monk singing out to his God, not-two.

Swāmī Abhishiktānanda was a mystic, and like all mystics he struggled to put his experience and reflections, his intuitions, into words, and he was rarely satisfied with the result—for who can name God? Because of the inherent problem of ineffability in the mystical experience—Trinitarian, Advaitic, or both—Swāmī Abhishiktānanda turned to poetry as many mystics before him had, as he attested in the letter to his sister quoted above. Writing of his experience with Swāmī Ajātānanda in a letter to Odette Baumer-Despeigne dated May 22, 1973, he says tellingly:

> I found your letter at Rishikesh after the marvelous days of solitude with Marc in the *ashram* of Phulchatti. Three weeks totally given over to reading the Upanishads, filled with graces. I understood there that the Upanishad is a secret which is only properly given in the secret of the communication of the guru to the disciple.
>
> To write? For this which is beyond, theology does not suffice, poetry or its equivalent is needed. There is need of inspiration in the fullest sense. For the moment it is necessary "to return" from Phulchatti and for the body to regain itself. It is too overpowering to feel oneself in the presence of the True, and how can one express in words that which words would only betray?[20]

While one does not want to draw a hard and fast distinction between all forms of prose and of poetry, surely the logical and syntactic continuity assumed in many prose genres was less well suited to his deepest experiences than the associative and syntactic discontinuity of poetry. Swāmī Abhishiktānanda's attraction to poetry was akin to that of his great predecessor in the Catholic mystical tradition, St. John of the Cross (whom he cited with regularity). Here, John of the Cross explains his own verse project to an eager interlocutor:

> These stanzas, Reverend Mother, were obviously composed with a certain burning love of God. The wisdom and charity of God is so vast, as the Book of Wisdom states, that it reaches from end to end [Wis. 8:1], and the soul informed and moved by it bears in some way this very abundance and impulsiveness in her words. . . . It would be foolish to think that expressions of love arising from mystical understanding, like these stanzas, are fully explainable. The Spirit of the Lord, who abides in us and aids our weakness, as St. Paul says [Rom. 8:26], pleads for us with unspeakable groanings in order to manifest what we can neither fully understand nor comprehend.
>
> Who can describe in writing the understanding he gives to loving souls in whom he dwells? And who can express with words

---

20. Cited in Baumer-Despeigne, "Spiritual Way," 22–23.

the experience he imparts to them? Who, finally, can explain the desires he gives them? Certainly, no one can! Not even they who receive these communications. As a result these persons let something of their experience overflow in figures, comparisons and similitudes, and from the abundance of their spirit pour out secrets and mysteries rather than rational explanations.[21]

The free-verse meditations Swāmī Abhishiktānanda left to posterity are superlatively religious, and, often, superlatively erotic. There is a pregnant longing for both consummation and annihilation pervading Swāmī Abhishiktānanda's poems that is a concentrated version of the same longing present in all his writings. Of course, in this marriage, the Swāmī is in good company with mystics of every generation and culture, and representatives of at least many of the world's religions—from the Song of Songs to Rumi and Hafez, from John of the Cross to Swāmī Abhishiktānanda's beloved Shrī Ramana Maharshi. In this (not unexpectedly), Swāmī Abhishiktānanda and his work have an intimately Christian/monastic appeal as well as a cross-cultural and interreligious one. If we are to read these poems well, we must take them in the existential and intensely transformational spirit, found across religions and cultural perspectives, in which they were composed. John of the Cross again:

> If these similitudes are not read with the simplicity of the spirit of knowledge and love they contain, they will seem to be absurdities rather than reasonable utterances, as will those comparisons of the divine Song of Solomon and other books of Sacred Scripture where the Holy Spirit, unable to express the fullness of his meaning in ordinary words, utters mysteries in strange figures and likenesses. The saintly doctors, no matter how much they have said or will say, can never furnish an exhaustive explanation of these figures and comparisons, since the abundant meanings of the Holy Spirit cannot be caught in words. Thus the explanations of these expressions usually contains less than what they embody in themselves.[22]

The Texts

In preparing this translation, I have utilized a variety of sources. Most importantly, presented here for the first time are complete versions of

---

21. John of the Cross, "Spiritual Canticle," 469.
22. John of the Cross, "Spiritual Canticle," 469–70.

the poems Swāmī Abhishiktānanda himself prepared for publication as stand-alone collections. During his time at Arunāchala and after, Swāmī Abhishiktānanda worked on a monograph in which he tried to articulate his growing perspectives on the interaction of Christianity and Hinduism in India and in his own heart. Included in this work, entitled *Guhāntara* ("the dweller in the cave of the heart"), were several poems he had composed during his time at Arunāchala. Throughout the 1950s, Swāmī Abhishiktānanda attempted to find acceptance for *Guhāntara* from his European censors and from others in his ever-widening circle. Though most of the essays in *Guhāntara* would be published in two of his later volumes, the collection as he had prepared it has yet to be presented to the public. Some of the poems from this period (and excerpts from them) were published in later volumes as well, but much of this material has sat in two typescripts prepared in 1960 and 1968 respectively and is currently housed in the archives of the Abhishiktānanda Centre for Interreligious Dialogue in Delhi, India. Swāmī Abhishiktānanda titled this strictly poetic collection "*Guhāntara*: In the Heart of Arunāchala" (1968). With the gracious encouragement and cooperation of Swāmī Ātmānanda Udāsīn and the Centre, I was granted access to these French typescripts and other primary texts, and I have prepared the translation in the first two sections of this volume directly from them.

Though I have translated and presented all the poems in these typescripts in the first two sections here, the two sets overlap substantially in material, and I have opted to keep Swāmī Abhishiktānanda's original poems from these two collections together and placed his "renderings" of Shrī Ramana Maharshi's poems, dispersed among his original poems in the 1960 typescript, in their own section to avoid confusion. The second collection, prepared in 1968, represents Swāmī Abhishiktānanda's final known work with these early poems. In light of this fact, I have followed this later typescript's order as the opening section to this volume. I have also retained the later readings presented there (except where noted), since he revised these poems for the final compilation. Though there are a few passages that were substantially overhauled, most of the revisions were minor in scope. As this is not a critical edition, I have not noted all instances where the typescripts differ. In the second section, Swāmī Abhishiktānanda's "renderings" of Shrī Ramana Maharshi's poems are presented in the order in which they appear in the 1960 typescript, but removed from their placement amidst Swāmī Abhishiktānanda's original poems there. While the integrity of the combination of the two groups of poems in the 1960 typescript is

Introduction

important, I did not collate the 1960 and 1968 typescripts together due to the logistical hurdle of combining all the pieces in a clear and transparently meaningful way. I hope that the appearance of Swāmī Abhishiktānanda's renderings of Shrī Ramana Maharshi's poems immediately after the opening section and before the remainder of his poems emphasizes the formative influence Shrī Ramana had on Swāmī Abhishiktānanda in the period of the original poems' composition and beyond. The importance of Shrī Ramana, the community of Shrī Ramana's āshram, and the holy mountain Arunāchala itself on Swāmī Abhishiktānanda at this time in his life cannot be overemphasized.

For the remaining two sections, I have included poems present in Swāmī Abhishiktānanda's prose works. These latter are primarily Swāmī Abhishiktānanda's spiritual diary—written over the course of his entire time in India and published posthumously by his friends—and his letters. Where parts of the poems presented in the first two sections of this volume appear in Swāmī Abhishiktānanda's diary, I do not reproduce them in the diary section. The poems contained in Swāmī Abhishiktānanda's letters are set off clearly by being centered on the page. However, the poems from his diary and other prose works are almost all in his free verse form containing long lines, and determining precisely where his thought and style shift from his diary entries' usual informal prose into the poetic mode is at times impressionistic. I can only beg the reader's indulgence in my decisions where to begin and end several of these, and admit that other translators may have started and ended at different points. Throughout, when entire poems or excerpts have appeared in print before, I provide this information either in section headings, titles, or footnotes.

The Present Translation

The task before the translator of poetry (over against the maker of the prose "crib" of poems in another language) is of course impossible. To carry the intimate association of lexical meaning, sonic embodiment, and other formal features characteristic of one language's poetry into those of another has long been recognized as a fool's errand. And yet, just as certainly, we make the attempt, for we hope that there is some aspect of the original that can come over into another language's poetic conventions and suggest to the attentive reader/auditor the poetic nature of the original. It seems to me that this predicament is analogous to Swāmī Abhishiktānanda's own desire to speak of what is beyond words, and I take comfort in following his lead to some small degree.

Thankfully, the relative proximity of modern French and English in both historical linguistics and poetic tradition attenuate this difficulty somewhat. In addition, Swāmī Abhishiktānanda's free verse circumvents any need on the translator's part to attempt to reflect formal features like rhyme or meters that are intrinsically related to line-by-line structure. Rather, his verse relies on stark images and their repetition and variation; syntactic breaks and units of thought related intimately to line breaks; and repeated syntactic structures, all of which can be transposed into modern English with a greater or lesser degree of equivalence.

Of course, French still employs its own idioms and turns of phrase, possesses its own density in certain expressions and prolixity in others relative to English. Throughout, I have elected to make these translations idiomatic in modern English while remaining as close to the original lineation and content as possible. Nevertheless, this does not mean that these poems are always and everywhere readily accessible, and they still possess strange images and turns of phrase, which are simply intrinsic to the mystical and unitive content Swāmī Abhishiktānanda treats so passionately and unhesitatingly.

In a similar vein, I have opted not to imitate the at-times archaic diction and word choice Swāmī Abhishiktānanda employs throughout his poems. While some would likely criticize this choice for its lack of fidelity to Swāmī Abhishiktānanda's stylistic *modus operandi*, I adopt here Edwin Morgan's defense of omitting intentional archaizing in his 1952 translation of *Beowulf*. In his approach to the deliberately archaizing language of the *Beowulf*-poet, Morgan claimed that the archaic nature of the poem's content (warriors, tribal kings, dragons, etc.) would provide a great enough sense of alienness for its modern audience to make "welkins" and "byrnies" unnecessary. Here, I suggest that the poetic outpourings of a Benedictine Advaitic mystic, couched in love imagery and Hindu religious terms and concepts, are distant enough from many contemporary readers' day-to-day experience to warrant not making the language unnecessarily opaque with "thee's" and "thou's" and other older language. To my mind, such an approach would only make these poems more difficult of access than they are likely to be already without adding substantial aesthetic appeal. Simplicity and clarity of phrase have been my watchwords wherever possible.

Introduction

Regarding the transliteration of Sanskrit words, I have not adopted the full range of markings for indicating Sanskrit sounds, as this is not a book for specialists in Sanskrit language. However, since Sanskrit is a language that makes phonemic distinctions based on long and short vowels, I have adopted the customary use of macrons to indicate long vowels.

Finally, wherever Swāmī Abhishiktānanda inserted notes in his text, I have prefaced these with the introductory tag "Author's Note." My own note within the body of the text is prefaced with the introductory tag "Translator's Note." All material in the footnotes is the translator's—Swāmī Abhishiktānanda did not provide footnotes to his poems.

With all these caveats and justifications, I hope that a faithful semblance of Swāmījī's voice appears in these pages, a reasonably clear witness to his vision of the not-two in the cave of the human heart.

Guhāntara: In the Heart of Arunāchala

Arunāchala

Author's Note

ARUNĀCHALA IS A HOLY place of particular veneration in Tamil Nadu in the South of India. The Puranas (Hindu scriptures comparable to Genesis) tell of its origins. There was a quarrel between Brahmā and Vishnu, each claiming that he was the First and Greatest. Suddenly, a Column of Fire appeared in the space between them. They decided that whoever first found either the foundation or the summit of this mysterious Column would be accepted by the other as the superior. Brahmā dashed to the summit, while Vishnu began to dig into the earth, but both had to admit the vanity of their efforts. It was Shiva who had manifested himself to them, convincing them of the futility of their former claims, for the greatest and first in Being is Shiva. The Column of Fire later turned into a Mountain of sapphire, and finally a Mountain of stone. Each year during the full moon of the month of Kārttikai (15 November–15 December), an immense fire is lit on the summit of the Mountain, which is called the feast of *Dīpam* ("dīpa" in Sanskrit; "lamp" in English). The Tamil name for the city there is Tiruvannamalai.[1]

> Arunāchala is a symbol.
> Arunāchala is a reality.
> A peak in Dravidian lands,
> glowing red—*arunā*—rising up in the sun's rays.
> Where we venerate the *Linga* of Fire,
> elemental sign of the living God,
> who appeared in the bush
> and on Horeb:[2]
> the consuming Fire, the Fire that enlightens:
> *Deus Ignis consumens*,[3]

---

1. [As noted in the Introduction, all material in the footnotes is provided by the translator.] "Tiru" is an honorific title in Tamil for "the holy one," equivalent to "Shrī" in Sanskrit; "annamalai" is a Tamil word composed of "malai" (mountain) and "anna" (powerful).

2. Exod 3:2; Deut 4:10–12.

3. "*Deus Ignis consumens*": "God, a consuming fire" (Latin); see Deut 4:24; Heb 12:29.

In the Bosom of the Father

Lux Mundi,[4]
Param-Jyoti,
Phôs hilaron,[5]
the joyous light of undying Glory
belonging to the Blessed One—
Bhagavan.

For this very light stood in ancient times,
this Column of Fire
whose summit Brahmā could not find,
nor Vishnu its base,
a Symbol of unfathomable love—
Anbé Shiva,
you who are the Depths of being!

Later, the Column turned to sapphire.
In our own sad time,
this *Kali yuga,*
the *Linga* of Fire turned to stone
to aid humanity,
the sacred Mountain—
achala—
whose base the Lord secured,
that will not shake.

To its caves, in every era,
those hungry for wisdom and renunciation come,
following one another,
the Mountain luring them
into its bosom with divine love
to teach them, in silence,
the royal road of incomparable Silence[6]

---

4. "*Lux Mundi*": "Light of the World" (Latin); see John 8:12.

5. "*Phôs hilaron*": "O gracious Light" (Greek); the first two words of an ancient Greek hymn still in use, especially in the Orthodox churches.

6. "royal road": cf. the *via regia* "royal way" of western Christian monastic thought as well as the yogic concept of *Rāja Yoga*, "royal path" of yoga.

and stability in the Self—[7]
*achala
ātmanishtha.*

Upon its sides flow springs
powerful in name—
"sacred pool of the Milk of Grace,"[8]
"milk of the divine Mother's breast"[9]—
where pilgrims
plunge and drink intently.

And then, on the great day of *Dīpam,* upon its summit,
when the sun sinks in the West
and the full moon rises over the horizon
in *Kārttikai,*
the column of Fire springs up,
freeing the secret of Light
hidden within the Mountain!

*
* *

Out from the depths
of Arunāchala's Heart,
the Source wherefrom its Waters and Light spring up,
from the secret of its Heart—
where those who are alone dwell in secret—
a message ever makes itself heard.
Or, at very least,
it seems it was whispered mysteriously
in that wondrous solitude
without and within,

---

7. "the Self": this is Swāmī Abhishiktānanda's first reference in the *Guhāntara* collection to the concept of "the Self" (Sanskrit: *Ātman*), a notion central to Advaita Vedantic philosophy. It is "the Self" who realizes "the Self" in liberation (Sanskrit: *moksha*).

8. "the sacred pool of the Milk of Grace": a spring on Arunāchala, called *Arutpāl Tīrtha* (Tamil).

9. "the milk of the breast of the divine Mother": a spring on Arunāchala, called *Mulaippāl Tīrtha* (Tamil).

In the Bosom of the Father

in the Depths,
in the Heart of Arunāchala.

But who can ever understand that message
coming from the Depths,
from the Heart of Arunāchala?
No one can discern it
who remains a stranger to what is within.
In the silence they will not hear
the OM Arunāchala whispers.
And who can explain it to them?
For them it is a book sealed
with the Seven Seals of the Apocalypse.[10]
Have even they known how to hear it
who dare to mumble it?
who dare to repeat
and attempt to express
what they hear within?
the eternal Silence
from within the Depths,
of the Heart of Arunāchala,
wherein the "I" the creature speaks
has sunk,
the secret place wherefrom it rises,
unique and alone?
Such is the mysterious Flame
that burns on the summit of Arunāchala
in the dark of *Dīpam*,
after the Sun that illumines the world has disappeared—
the three-fold, incomparable *AHAM* of divine Silence.[11]

*
* *

---

10. "Seven Seals of the Apocalypse": the Book (or Scroll) of the Seven Seals is first mentioned and described in Rev 5, while the opening of the Seals and the aftermath of each is related in Rev 6–11.

11. "the eternal Silence . . . and alone" and "the three-fold . . . divine Silence": excerpted for "Ehieh Asher Ehieh," in *Intériorité et révélation*, 87.

Without a doubt, those sages will lament
who do not find what they desire:
well-made theories,
their learned books' pleasing formulas,
the handsome shape of their thoughts.
But the formulas and theories
and fine literature—
can they reveal that message,
so simple in its purity,
unyielding in its nakedness,
that comes from the Depths,
from the Heart of Arunāchala?

At first, Hindus rejoiced:
the Barbarians from the West
have been drawn into the Depths
of Arunāchala's Heart,
drunk deeply of its waters,
bathed in its light,
hidden in its hollows.
But soon they will turn away,
no longer listening to the message
coming from the very depths
of the Heart of Arunāchala,
for they have not yet seen
that Christ is the Fulfillment of the Vedas
and that in the very depths of the caves of Arunāchala
the path leading to the Heart of Christ
opens up.

And Christians will perhaps become angry,
crying, "Sacrilege!"
when they hear that India's Sages and Rishis
here are heard and venerated
as Job and Melchizedek were—[12]

---

12. "Job and Melchizedek": Job is described as a man living in the Land of Uz (Job 1:1) while Melchizedek is the king of Salem and priest of the most high God (Gen 14:18–20), and so traditionally neither is seen as of the people of Israel, though they each have

those prophets of the Most High,
heralds of his advent
who did not belong to the people of the Covenant—
those whom God here clothed
in the lone Majesty of *Kevala*,
that here the Christian mysteries are meditated upon
in words and ideas intended
to resonate with India's inmost depths,
that the wondrous myths its heart devised
here serve to prefigure,
reveal, and manifest
the wondrous secret that reveals the Father's Heart
in Jesus his beloved Son,
the Anointed and Consecrated,
Shrī Abhishikta Īshvara,[13]
Christ, the sole Lord.
For many of them—alas!—have not yet understood:
within the Depths,
in the Heart of Arunāchala,
a unique jewel was hidden
by divine Wisdom
from ancient times
to await Christianity.
And they alone will find it
who have bathed in the waters of baptism,
been confirmed in the fires of the Spirit,
and will have dared to enter
into the Depths
of the Heart of Arunāchala.

*

* *

---

a prophetic role in Christian salvation history.

13. "*Shrī Abhishikta Īshvara*": "the Blessed Anointed Lord" (Sanskrit); "Abhishikta" ("Anointed") and "Īshvara" (Lord) being the terms used to form the initial *sannyāsi* name of Swāmī Abhishiktānanda, Swāmī Abhishikteshvarānanda. This line is present in some manuscripts but not the final; given its significance in Swāmī Abhishiktānanda's life, I have retained it here.

What matter now who passes on the message—
the voiceless call within the Depths
of the Heart of Arunāchala—
to those who hasten to the Depths
of the Heart of Arunāchala?
For they enter into the Depths
of the Heart of Arunāchala,
and have they not lost even their names
and all that was until that moment,
that they might be nothing more
than those who live in the Depths,
Guhāntara—
those who live within the Cave
of the Heart of Arunāchala?

Blessed are they who receive the message
coming from the Depths
of the Heart of Arunāchala,
within the Depths
in the Heart of Arunāchala,
entering into their own Depths,
sunk into the Self,
who find in their own inmost depths
the secret of Arunāchala.

But for those who embark
on the descent to the Depths
of the Heart of Arunāchala,
all will soon vanish below the horizon
except Arunāchala.
For Arunāchala is a harsh Guru
vanquishing everything
one loved before,
everything
one enjoyed before,
everything
that supported one before:
things of this world and of the other,

even the joy
found in the love of God and others.
He leaves them suspended,
free and naked,
in the solitude of *Kevala*
there in the abyss
within the Depths
in the Heart of Arunāchala.[14]

And for those who finally touch the Depths
of the Heart of Arunāchala,
are there still depths?
is there still an Arunāchala?
Where has the Mountain gone,
glowing-red Arunāchala?
where have the Springs gone
upon the sides of Arunāchala?
What has become of the Light
upon the summit of Arunāchala?
The very caves disappear
for the recluses of Arunāchala.
Have they not themselves vanished,
sunk in the Depths
of the Heart of Arunāchala,
gone in the Self?
Forever lost in the Depths:
the Incomparable Arunāchala![15]

*
* *

Kārttikai/December 26, 1953
Cave of Arutpāl Tīrtha, Arunāchala

14. "For Arunāchala ... of Arunāchala": excerpted for *Souvenirs d'Arunâchala* (1978), 58 and translated in *The Secret of Arunâchala* (1979), 36.

15. "Arunāchala is ... the Mountain"; "From within ... of Arunāchala"; and "And for ... Incomparable Arunāchala!": a slightly different version of these passages was excerpted for *Souvenirs d'Arunâchala* (1978), 77–80 and translated in *The Secret of Arunâchala* (1979), 51–54.

Poems Inspired by Tamil Verses

Arunāchala—
within the Depths
in the final
Darkness
of the Crypt:
a solitary
Flame.

Who will dare tell the secret
that hides the Flame
in its Closeness?
the mystery of Being?
the mystery of Three?

That one alone will know
but will never repeat,
who, fallen into that Flame
and entirely consumed,
is nothing but Flame.[16]

December 26, 1953

—

ARUNĀCHALA—
the Mountain that calls,
saying within: "Come, but come now!
you whose hearts
thirst after wisdom
and have renounced all."[17]

---

16. "Arunāchala, within . . . but Flame": slightly different versions of this poem appear in *Souvenirs d'Arunâchala* (1979), 83 (translated in *The Secret of Arunâchala* [1979], 57) and in "Ehieh Asher Ehieh" in *Intériorité et révélation* (1982), 102.

17. "ARUNĀCHALA—the . . . renounced all": a free rendering of lines traditionally ascribed to the fifteenth-century sage Gurunamashivaya, who lived at Arunāchala. The

Salvation is for those who die in Benares.
Salvation is for those who are born at Tiruvarur.
Salvation is for those too who worship at Chidambaram.
But salvation is the more sure
for those who simply call to mind
the holy Mountain of Arunāchala.
For Arunāchala is thrice-holy,
the very memory of which is enough
to obtain liberation at once![18]

—

Arunāchala, the *Linga* of Fire:
luminous Column standing
higher than all the heavens,
deeper than the depths of the earth,
in the very spaces of my heart![19]

*
* *

---

original lines are given in French in *Souvenirs d'Arunâchala* (1978), 137 and translated into English in *The Secret of Arunâchala* (1979), 103.

18. "Salvation is . . . at once": a free rendering of traditional lines, which are given in French in *Souvenirs d'Arunâchala* (1978), 137 and are translated into English in *The Secret of Arunâchala* (1979), 103.

19. "Arunâchala, the . . . my heart": this poem appears in *Souvenirs d'Arunâchala* (1978), 83 and is translated in *The Secret of Arunâchala* (1979), 57.

Bhairava[20]

Why have you attacked me so violently, O Arunāchala?
You've burned me, wounded me.
>In your grace finish me off, You who are so Cruel!
>You've left me lame, shaking—my flesh rots
>from the wounds you've laid upon me,
>>O Arunāchala!

I can't walk, cannot move,
>lying here, there, before you:
>>and you just laugh.

You have ravished me, Arunāchala,
like a virgin you've spoken words of love to.
And you left me lying here,
>there, before you.
>They all look at me

and laugh,[21] those who pass by and catch sight of me.
>No one will have anything to do with me,
>>for you have visited me,
>>>O Arunāchala!

You who have ravished me: take me at last,
>or finish me off.
>You who have wounded me, kill me,
>or, if not, then heal me!

You who have burned me, consume me,
>or at least come and burn with me.
>You laugh at me,

left me alone, naked and lying here,
>there, before you.

---

20. Sections of this poem appear in *La montée au fond du cœur* (1986), 203–5, 223–24, and 225, and are translated in *The Ascent to the Depth of the Heart* (1998), 163–64 and 181–83.

21. "They look . . . and laugh": cf. Ps 22:7.

In the Bosom of the Father

You've snatched me up, Aruṇāchala,
        seizing me,
    my clothing, ornaments, everything,
            promising me everything . . .
And You haven't even kissed me.

Your face brushed up against me, Your arms drew closer,
and I stretched out my lips, reached out my arms.
        And You, You laughed at me,
        retreated into your mystery—
        Inaccessible!

    And I continue lying here, naked, there,
no longer possessing the strength to stand.
        And I am sunk in shame.
    I won't even look at myself . . .
All this is Your doing, O Aruṇāchala.
    I don't even want to think of You.

        I want to abandon You,
    to leave You here,
        as You've left me,
           leaving Your memory behind—
           and so take my revenge!
    Alas, You have eaten away at my heart,
and the worm left there gnaws it, gnaws it terribly,
        and I can't tear it out.
        No, I can't tear You out!

        To forget You, I long, I'm trying . . .
        Ah! how to forget You?
        Since You forget me?
    It's as if Your heart were inside me,
           O Deceiver.
        You should not call out to me,
        if You refuse to give yourself to me.

Deceiver, Destroyer:
You are *Natarāja* the Dancer too,
who tramples me.
You dance and You, You make fun of me,
with every step You change form,
You from whom all forms proceed!

*
* *

You've snatched me up again, Arunāchala,
now You want to snatch up my very self.
Will You even devour my flesh,
    You Ogre?

Will You then make me a beggar, dressed in only some string and a rag between my legs, passing the night under one of the porticos of Your Temple and going off to a village every morning to beg my pittance of rice in a chipped bowl—with a shaggy beard, flea-ridden hair, sitting all day long in the courtyards of Your sanctuary, fixed only on You, Arunāchala, my eyes fixed on Your summit, there where the *Dīpam* shoots forth on the sacred day of *Kārttikai* and wherefrom You forever dart out in Your surging Flame, devouring the hearts of Your devotees? Or will You hide me in one of the rocky hollows at the foot of Your mountain, Arunāchala, in the darkness of Your caverns, penetrating even to You, to the last crevice of its heart?

    For You only give Yourself to those who've given up everything,
        O Arunāchala—
        stripped of bodies
        stripped of hearts
        stripped of spirits
        stripped of very selves—
those from whom You've taken everything, everything that could possibly still say: "I."

And so, down the centuries, You've lured many,
    a Magnet,
toward Your Temple, toward Your caves,

toward Your summit of stone and fire,
toward Your bright springs.
       And You've brought so many, panting—
          O Deceiver!—
prostrate to Your feet, to the hollows of Your heart, having disappeared,
         and You keep them—moaning, roaring,
              quivering at the call to Your grace![22]

                *
           *   *

Arunāchala, the Flame shining out from Your summit,
    as I walk along, contemplating You
        in the sacred night of *Dīpam*,
    finishing my circuitous pilgrimage,
the full moon of *Kārttikai* also turns about you,
        finishing in the firmament above
           its own heavenly *giri-pradakshinā*.

    How burdensome it is to make someone perform the mundane human task
when once he has been marked by Arunāchala,
when the Light of Love and the Dawn, *Aruna*, has burst forth in the depths of his heart,
    when he has been established like a mountain, *achala*, unshakable,

      or the Column of Fire, whose foundation and summit
      I've no better chance of finding than Brahmā and Perumal:
      where it begins (if it begins), where it ends (if it ends).
    For he snatches me from this time that passes along,
from the shining day that wanes,
from this moment that disappears,
    from all the past and all the future,
      taking from me, snatching away every memory and desire,
      and I no longer know where I am, from where I have come,
nor where I will go, nor where I am set,

---

22. "For You . . . Your grace!": these lines are excerpted for *Souvenirs d'Arunâchala* (1978), 83–84 and *The Secret of Arunâchala* (1979), 57–58.

for he has driven his endless foundation into my heart,
a Column of Fire that blinds and burns me,
and I know nothing, not of myself, nor of the world, nor of God,
nothing about that radiant light without ray, without reflection,
without any line at all where the eye could rest, begin to measure it,
where everything is light, before and behind, above and below,
    without size or shape, the uncircumscribable Sea of its
    Glory—

    an icy sea without limit, where one is taken
    for good,
tender and heartrending at once,
    at least, while there still remains something to be
        consumed
    by this Fire,
    the ray of darkness.

                                November, 1955
                            Mauna Mandir, Kumbakonam

Beyond the Depths

Beyond the depths,
beyond being,
beyond the present moment,
beyond the self,
beyond the *AHAM*,
beyond the OM,
beyond all that human thought can achieve,
beyond all that humanity can or believes it can achieve by not thinking,

beyond all that manifests
and all that is manifest,
beyond all times and their origins,
beyond all times and their fulfillments,
where there is no more time
nor non-time,

where Arunāchala is no more,
nor the Light at its Summit,
glances to contemplate its flame without,
glances to contemplate its flame within,
the spring on its side,
lips to drink its waters outwardly,
lips to drink within,
its rocky hollows
or the OM it utters,
unique and solitary,
in the hearts of those who live there,
silent and solitary,
nor the Flame that shoots up
in the bosom of those who live there,
naked and solitary
in the secret of the Darkness,

the mystery of the primordial *avyakta*,
the silence before the beginning
that is the Father
before he becomes manifest in his Son—
calling out within himself:
AHAM, AHAM—
and his Word, *Vāk*, became flesh,
bringing together in himself
the world here below
and the worlds above,
bringing to fulfillment between his wailing in Bethlehem
and his cry upon the Cross
all that he had uttered within to humanity,
audible and inaudible,
from ancient times
within the Depths,
in the Heart of Arunāchala,

the mystery of the final *avyakta*,
the last silence
that is the Spirit
once everything has returned to the Father
in the Son,
with the Son himself—
the outward sign will be put off
for eternity.

Who can speak of Silence's secret,
the *avyakta*,
the mystery of *Vāk*,
the mystery of *AHAM*,
the mystery of OM,
the mystery of One and of Three,
the mystery of not-two, of not-one?

They alone know it
but will never repeat it,
who have plunged into Silence,

have themselves become forever
and always
the Silence,
who in days past have resounded
within the Depths,
in the Heart of Arunāchala,

*
* *

Is not the whole mystery of India
and her Rishis, those predestined witnesses of the *avyakta*,
the mystery from the Depths,
the secret of the Heart of Arunāchala,
of its Flame turned to stone and its rocky hollows,
the long preparation for the Word and the Spirit
simply fixing oneself in the Self—
achala
ātmanishta—
and plunging ever more within
from depths to depths
until for her everything has passed away:
what is seen, heard, or thought
and what no longer thinks,
every "Manifestation,"
every Epiphany of God
on the earth
and in the heavens,
gone into eternal
Silence,

so that she will ever be within Holy Church
(the Church of Silence),
which lives within the Depths
in the secret from within
the *Guhā*,
Guhāntara,
in the Darkness

where God shows himself
an Epiphany
to Himself
and to humanity
in the essential Silence
of the Father's bosom:

where Jesus entered,
as soon as he came into existence
in the first awakening of his Consciousness
to BEING

Dominus dixit ad me:
Filius meus es TU
EGO hodie genui TE.[23]

December 21, 1953
Arunāchala

---

23. "*Dominus dixit . . . genui TE*": "The Lord said to me, 'YOU are my Son; I have begotten YOU this day" (Latin); see Ps 2:7; Acts 13:33; Heb 1:5.

The Other Shore[24]

They found him on the other shore . . . (John 6:25)

1. Ascent to the Source

"The ascent to the Source," "crossing to the Other Shore"—all images handed down by our Fathers to lead humanity by the road of symbols to the inmost realities.

The return to origins, the reaching of every fulfillment.

Life is an ascent, a crossing, a Passover.
Only enough time to set a foot down. Ever departing. Beyond.
We live in going outside ourselves.
We reach ourselves by losing ourselves.
And so, in the Hindu myth Shiva is the Great Liberator precisely because he is the Great Destroyer, the One who dances in the cremation grounds, wearing about his neck a garland of skulls, that symbol of Death, which severs everything from life—
Shiva, the Benevolent One, upon whom the Upanishads meditate. Shiva, who is Love, *Anbé* Shiva, as Tirumular, the Tamil saint, sang.
He who strips everything away, who forbids us to remain in anything that *is* not, who ceaselessly makes what is only *becoming* to pass beyond.
He is Time, sweeping humanity and all the universe in its inexorable cycle away, mowing down the passing moment and bringing to birth the one that follows.
He keeps Life from standing still, keeps us from clinging to the present moment.
He breaks every attachment, unhooks every link,
every link holding humanity to this shore where we pretend to find happiness.

Shiva, who frees us from the passing moment by means of the Present.

---

24. A version of this poem was published in *Initiation à la spiritualité des Upanishads*, 31–34 and translated in *The Further Shore* (1984), 131–34.

For, in reality, is Being not always present? Origins are not found in a past that has been lost, but in the Now. And is the other shore not already reached?

Has not the voice that calls the dead to Life already sounded,[25] and has not the hour already arrived for us to worship God in spirit and truth?[26]

We struggle to find God and to find ourselves. And—alas!—we too often fail to find either.

We look for God in a small patch of space. But God fills all of space, completely outside of space.

We look for God in some point in time, a past that once was or a future that will yet be. But God is completely outside time, eternity present in each moment.

"The smallest abyss." We must leap just right, otherwise we'll miss our shot, and find ourselves further on, on an "other shore" that is not the true one.

God is close at hand, and so we constantly fail to reach him.
We make God an object, and he escapes us.
We make God a thought, but thought passes him by.
Thus the Magdalene was too preoccupied by the thought of Jesus to recognize him in the gardener of Mt. Calvary.[27]
And Cleopas too was so preoccupied with the memory of Jesus that he did not know it was he who accompanied him to Emmaus until Jesus made himself known.[28]
But, as he said to Thomas, blessed are those who know him at first sight![29]

Whoever has known him in himself has known him in all.
Whoever has known him in the Church, has known him in all that prepared for the Church.

---

25. "Has not . . . already sounded": John 5:25.
26. "has not . . . and truth": John 4:23.
27. See John 20:14–15.
28. See Luke 24:18.
29. "blessed are . . . first sight!": see John 20:29.

Everything is pure for those who are pure;[30] everything recalls the Spirit for one who has once been gently touched by the Spirit.

Without a doubt, he should be aware of the varieties of brilliance shining forth from the transfigured Lord.[31]

He knows that the fullness of Light only shone upon the earth when he took on flesh—he in whom, in the beginning, the Father said, "*Fiat Lux*, Let there be Light!"[32]

And he knows too that the Spirit was only given to humanity in his fullness after the Resurrection of the Lord.[33]

And yet, seeing him in all his signs, he cannot fail to know him and adore the One who is signified.

His faith makes up for the sign's lack. Or, rather, his faith itself gives the sign its truth.

The one who gazes at the midday sun afterward only sees the sun's glare. Likewise, every color is only a reflection of the sun. Even the darkness that rejects the light is a sign of the sun, for without the sun and its light the darkness could not exist and no one could see it.

The Lord is present everywhere. "His course extends from the East to the West."[34]

He is everywhere, He alone. And yet, though within all things, He is not any one of them.

But recognizing the Presence of the Lord and his Spirit everywhere makes our need to announce the Resurrection no less urgent, nor to carry everywhere the message:

"We have beheld His Glory, the Glory of the Only Son of the Father, filled with Grace and Truth!"[35]

Christ is the final goal of the World. If we are meant to work together with all our intelligence and all our physical strength for the enrichment of this world, promoting the bodily and mental growth of our brothers, we have the duty no less to take part, with all our strength and all the grace we've received, in the fulfillment of all things in this world in Christ and

---

30. "Everything is . . . are pure": Titus 1:15.
31. For the Transfiguration, see Matt 17:1-8; Mark 9:2-8; and Luke 9:28-36.
32. "*Fiat* lux . . . be light!": Gen 1:1.
33. For Pentecost and the Descent of the Holy Spirit, see Acts 2; for the Resurrection, see Matt 28; Mark 16; Luke 24; and John 20.
34. "His course . . . the West": Ps 19[18]:7.
35. "We have . . . and Truth": John 1:14.

in the ever more glorious advent of Christ in the heart and soul of every person.

No one has received a thing but to share it with his brothers.

The Church herself does not possess the Eucharist; she is at the service of the Eucharist. And she offers it only that the world may pass, in the Eucharist, from the sign it is to the reality it is called to be.

The faithful communicate only as ministers for creation.

The Christian then must communicate to his brothers the Glory he has received as gift. In him this Glory is the promise of its own manifestation. It only shines in him to the extent that it radiates around him.

But for the Christian to do this he must share this message with his brother where he already is, where the Spirit has led him, and, in him, where he awaits the Christian,
> in the depths of Arunāchala's cave,
> on the other shore of the self,
> at the Source!

Only there can he make known to his brother that in the depths of Arunāchala's cave, there also is the Heart of Christ,
> and that Source is the Bosom of the Father,
> the Other Shore,
> where Jesus awaits him!

2. Excerpts from the Upanishads[36]

"This is the bridge beyond death . . .
Salvation to all who pass to the other shore,
beyond the darkness!"

(Mundaka Upanishad 2.2.5–6)

"at the furthest edge of the beyond!"

(Katha Upanishad 3.1)

"So the blessed Sanatkumāra showed him
the other shore, beyond darkness,
and they call him Skanda, the one who jumps . . ."

(Chāndogya Upanishad 7.26.2)

"The One who establishes all things, inconceivable in form,
the color of the sun,
the One who is beyond the darkness."

(*Bhagavad Gītā* 8.9)

"Having taken the OM as a boat just large enough,
crossing over the space of your heart
and reaching the other shore,
the space within
that gradually becomes clear,
you will enter the palace of Brahman."

(Maitri Upanishad 6.28)

---

36. These excerpts were published in *Initiation à la spiritualité des Upanishads*, 35.

3. The Other Shore[37]

All our works are done to cross to the other shore,
    whether we know it or not.
He crosses in dream; he crosses in the world myth and symbol open up,
    in the world of signs that bear reality forth.

Just so, the Hebrews crossed over the Red Sea, over desert—a sea of another kind—
and the Jordan,
the one Moses himself could not cross . . .

He crosses to the heart's other shore in the great sacrament
    of the World, of Humanity.
Every person he meets, every being he brushes past is his Boatman,
    all that he sees in the events of the world, in human history
    or his own, outside him as well as within his own thoughts,
    is his crossing to the other shore of himself,
    to the depths of his self, inaccessible to his own consciousness.

    For "He is" other than himself,
other than all that appears as the self,
other than all that he thinks of the self,
other than all that can reach the self,
and this realization tears him apart,
ever since, like a flash of lightening, it illumined the abyss of his being,
and, like lightning, it has opened those depths in breaking them.
It is depth and breadth and height—
    who cares about the words scholars use to enclose
the mystery that lies within:
no one will understand who has not first seen it within himself—
    who at some point has experienced those beatific death throes.

The descent to the depths where there is no longer anything left of the self,
    rising up from that abyss to the Light and finding the Self:

---

37. The beginning and end of this poem appear in *Initiation à la spiritualité des Upanishads*, 36–38 and are translated in *The Further Shore* (1984), 135–38.

> the Passover!
> "Awakened," I find myself in You:
> > *resurrexi et adhuc tecum sum.*[38]

For "He is" other than the self; yet, if he is, is he not deep within the self?

> And people amuse themselves, occupy themselves, they make war, make love, make money, and the learned talk while the scribes make laws . . .

"I looked everywhere under the vault of heaven
> and saw only vanity,"
> > says Quoheleth.[39]

> The descent into Hell and rising again on Easter morning:

for we must descend to the depths of the abyss
to awaken on the other shore,
which possesses no other.
That "other" in my own depths which does not have an other:
> Being, the Self.

*
* *

But this other "shore," he must come there alone:
> naked as stone is naked
> naked as glass is naked
> naked as the self is naked.

He began this work in the sacrament of the World, continued it in the sacrament
> of Humanity, and ends it in the sacrament of the Church.

In the power of this final sacrament, he plunges
> into the abyss
> with his Faith.

---

38. "*resurrexi et . . . tecum sum*": "I arose and am still with you" (Latin); Ps 138[139]:18 and see the Entrance Antiphon for Easter Sunday in the pre- and post-Vatican II Roman Rite (*Roman Missal* [New York: Catholic Book Publishing, 1964]; *The Roman Missal* [Collegeville, MN: Liturgical Press, 2011].

39. "I looked . . . says Quoheleth": Eccl 1:14. "Quoheleth" is the pseudonym for the speaker of the book of Ecclesiastes.

But there he has lost everything:
>every covering, every ornament,
>all that has hidden him from himself,
>adorning or veiling.

Everything is torn away:
>the very body in death,
>even the joy of feeling loved by God—
>*Deus meus ut quid me dereliquisti*[40]—
>O Father, why have you abandoned me?
>Left by man, left by God,
>>Alone with the self,
>Alone, alone without end.

There he found the solitude of the Alone,
the Solitude of Being,
the joy of BEING, the peace of Being, the freedom of Being.

He awoke: there was no more abyss, no more river, no more shore.
Arunāchala had vanished,
"He was."

>>To pass to the other bank,
>>to the other shore of the heart,
>words are the boatman, as well as thoughts,
>>the mind is the boat just big enough.

>>But he fell in between
>>>in the Self.

For he was caught in a whirlwind, and was no longer
>downstream or upstream, neither above nor below, in Heaven nor

the abyss, not on the shore, lacking size and shape—
>>in endless space.
>And so he came to the other shore.

>>>Having reached the midpoint,
>>>he plunged all the way down to the Depths.

---

40. "*Deus meus . . . me derelequisti*: "My God, why have you abandoned me?" (Latin); Ps 22[21]:1; Matt 27:46; Mark 15:34.

In the Bosom of the Father

*
* *

     It is the OM I utter,
          the utterance of that OM,
the knowledge I have that I utter it,
the consciousness I have to know this,
the consciousness of this consciousness . . .
       at the last
   nothing else remains,
     so it is HIM.
     AHAM, I am!
The one who sees, the *sākshī*, the Witness, longs to stay 'til the end, to see the Other
    appear.
He does not assent to getting involved in the crossing, nor to ride on the boat.
But while his feet remain planted on this shore, it would blind him to scan
     the other side, and he will never know "the other shore,"
for the other shore is on the other side of himself,
in himself, outside himself, finally in himself,
in the self, outside the self, finally in the Self!

* * *
* * * *

    There is a mystery present in every thing,[41]
    a mystery present in the world,
    and it is humanity who sets the secret of this mystery free,
    the secret of being, coming forth from the Father.

    There is a mystery in every person,
    and it is Christ who reveals this mystery to each person
        in their own depths—
    there where they awaken eternally to themselves
        in the Father's Depths.

---

41. "There is . . . of God": this passage appears in *La montée au fond du cœur*, 232–33 and was translated in *The Ascent to the Depth of the Heart*, 189–90.

> There is a mystery in every people,
> and it is the Church who discloses to each people its own mystery,
> the fruitful Spirit in its own depths
> overshadowing each like Mary,
> for in each the Word is also born
> from the Father's Depths.

There is a mystery in India . . .

What our Rishis realized concerning Being in the depths of the self,
   overshadowed by the Spirit,
what they, moved by his Breath,
uttered concerning Being, what they found in the depths of the self,
what in the depths of the heart our Rishis pronounced concerning the self,
   Vāk, the eternal Word,

that same Word that came in human flesh, with a human soul,
revealing all that was hidden about humanity—
as much as can be heard by human ears
   and related in words:
the fullest *brahmavidyā*, knowledge of the Father,
the fullest *ātmavidyā*, knowledge of the Spirit,
Wisdom itself: *Prajna Parāmitā*, and he revealed the secret of reaching him,
the Way of Faith, the Way of Love,
of reaching him in communion with others.

This was the OM our Rishis heard resounding in their souls
when they made the descent to their own depths,
deeper than their thoughts, deeper than all their desires
in the existential solitude of Being:

the OM resounding in the sound of leaves rustling in the wind,
the OM howling in the storm,
   moaning in the breeze,
the OM rushing in the raging flood
   and the sweetest sound of the river flowing calmly to the sea,
the OM following the spheres crisscrossing the firmament
and the OM throbbing at the atom's core.

The one singing the birds' songs,
crying the animals' cries in the forest,
the OM in human laughter and the OM in their sobbing,
the OM stirring in their thoughts and all their desires,
the OM in their words of war, love, exchange,
the OM that made Time and History in their passing,
the OM that made Space by entering into Time.

This OM, of a sudden, broke whole and entire into a small corner of space
and one moment in time
in his essential Fullness,
when the Son of Man was conceived in Mary's womb,
the Word, the Son of God.[42]

*
* *

In my soul I carry a mystery, my own mystery,[43]
the very mystery of Being.
And my whole concern on this earth is to name it—
that which is beyond all names,
those names that are things,
those names we've given to things,
those names, those words, that crisscross my mind in every direction
        and zigzag about like mad stars.
For this mystery is the mystery of my body,
of each part of my body, every member,
every part's curve, the smoothness of my skin,
the self-same mystery of my heart,
of my affections and desires,
expectations and regrets,
my refusals . . .
And this is the self-same mystery each of my brothers carries within themselves,

    42. "This was . . . of God": these lines appear in *Prayer* (1989), 115–16, translated from the French edition *Éveil à soi—éveil à Dieu* (1971), 129–30.

    43. "In my . . . has opened": this passage appears in *La montée au fond du cœur*, 219–21 and is translated in *The Ascent to the Depth of the Heart*, 177–79 (this translation omits the present passage's fifth line).

in their own bodies, their steps, their silence, their talk,
in their cares, their passions.
And this is the mystery I feel trembling in them when I touch them
or when I draw close to their souls.
And this is the self-same mystery present in the firmament,
in the very bowels of the sun and the heart of every star,
in the depths of the oceans,
in fire,
in the wind that blows,
in space—inexplicable, unknowable, irreducible—
in the earth that sustains those born of her:
    every plant, animal, and person.

And this is the mystery pervading history,
in the time people make, that measures their lives,
in time as the wind blows and fire consumes,
as the waters flow, streams into rivers, from mountains to oceans,
from the oceans to the firmament, and again to the bowels of the earth.
This is the mystery present in those who decide the fate of humanity, imposing
    their wills.
And it is at once the mystery residing in the hearts of the weakest
    of those born of woman, the humble
as well as those grand people who parade in the midst of the children of men.

And this mystery was not more present in the heart of Jesus of Nazareth,
    the eternal Word, incarnate in time and in the stuff of this world
than it is in my own heart.

For the mystery is one, *ekam eva advitīyam*,[44] indivisible,
    akhanda, and impenetrable, *asparsha*.

And the mystery is hidden—and at the same time
    revealed so boldly—in the secret of our Temples' dark sanctuaries
and in the bowels of the Mountain called Arunāchala,
    wherefrom the Waters well and the Flame springs up,
in the stone snakes the humble, in their piety, erect at the foot of trees,

---

44. "*ekam eva advitīyam*": "one without a second" (Sanskrit), being, an Advaitic teaching.

in the teaching of Rishis and the *darshana* of Gurus—
when we encounter them, the mystery rises so profoundly from the depths
of our hearts all the way to the depths of our hearts,
they dig deeper and deeper, mercilessly
into the pits of darkness wherefrom springs the splendor of Being.

In the heart of the Son of Mary this mystery
       revealed itself in its Fullness,
bringing forth the words that would lead us to him.
For Jesus is the Word itself,
       the *Logos*, *Vāk*,
and because he himself is the Word, he spoke.

*
* *

And still this inner mystery eats away at the heart
of the poor wretch wallowing in the mud,
in his vomit and excrement
of matter, heart, or thought—
the Spirit who burned and devoured
Job's heart, scratching himself upon the dung heap,
and the heart of Raikva, scratching himself under his cart,
who revealed the truth to King Bhallaksha,[45]
       the descendent of Jānashruta, so proud and self-satisfied
       in his good works and charity.
The mystery lies behind the dull eyes of the poor woman
       and the prostitute, struggling just to find food,
in the Cancalaise bawling and yelling at the fish market,[46]
behind the vanity of those who strut about
and drink praise as if it were sweet milk,

---

45. Presumably referring to King Jānashruti, the grandson of Jānashruta and the king who learns from Raikva in the fourth chapter of the Chāndogya Upanishad. Within this story, the term "Bhallaksha" is used by one swan (Sanskrit: *haṁsa*) to address another. It appears that Swāmī Abhishiktānanda has accidentally used this name in place of "Jānashruti."

46. "*Cancalaise*": a female inhabitant of Cancale in Brittany (French), where Swāmī Abhishiktānanda was born and began his monastic life. A rare incorporation of a common scene from Swāmī Abhishiktānanda's earlier life.

behind the pride and cunning and anger of men,
of those who guide the fate of the world
and those who will never leave their streets and slums,
just as it lies in the holiness and devotion and love of those who lead others
    to the life of the Spirit,
in the habit of the Sisters of Charity,
the complete selflessness of a mother,
the prayer of a child whose heart God has opened.

          *   *   *
        *   *   *   *

    God does not create for a particular end,[47]
        for God has no goal.
        He is because he is.
        He acts because he is.
        He creates all in being.

God creates in play, but not in order to play:
he does nothing for anything,
he is Play, as he is Being,
he is Being in its complete freedom,
its spontaneity that nothing can bind.
And this is no terrible thing for humanity:
    Natarāja dances, not because he wants to,
        but because he is.

The child who runs and jumps and sings
without knowing whereto he runs, nor what he sings, nor why he dances—
    what a wondrous thing!
The adult ever acts for a purpose, playing or resting.
Maturing, the adult forgets how wondrous it is to be,
    simply to be, without thought to more.
    The adult *wants* to be, and he *is becoming*.
    He does not know *being*.

---

    47. "God does ... Lord Natarāja": this passage appears in *La montée au fond du cœur*, 226 and is translated in *The Ascent to the Depth of the Heart*, 183–84.

In the Bosom of the Father

The child *is* and plays.
And so God plays in the world.

The adult asks God questions about how the world works:
why he did this and not that?
why he tossed us into *samsāra*?
what will happen tomorrow and years from now?

We are too serious a partner for God.

When Vishnu desired to come to earth as Krishna,
he made the somber ascetics of old
        take the form of shepherdesses
and he devoted himself to those men-become-women wholeheartedly,
playing with them, doing tricks for them, kissing them,
making them come before him completely naked,
naked and bursting with laughter, like children . . .
        So the Spirit plays in the world.
        "Play, jump, and dance with me
        in the *ākāsha* of your heart,"
        says Lord Natarāja.

*
* *

        In the depths of the self,
        where no foundation
        has been dug nor anything built
        by the hand or mind of man—
        deeper than anything dug by man,
    earlier and deeper than the arising of any desire,
    earlier and deeper than the arising of any symbol,
        image, or concept—
alone with the self, in the sources of one's being,
        alone with the Absolute,
        alone in the solitude of the Alone
        in the *Kevala* without name:
there, where the soul goes out from the Creator's hands,

outside him and in him all the same, he awakens to being:
that HE Alone Is.

December, 1956
Mauna Mandir, Kumbakonam

4. *(Awakening) In the Bosom of the Father*

> In the bosom of the Father[48]
> in his eternal awakening,
> in Mary's womb
> in his human awakening,
> in the bosom of the Church
> in his awakening in souls.
>
> In his Paschal awakening
> in the bosom of the Father,
> in his awakening in faith
> in the bosom of every soul,
> in his awakening in Glory
> in his final *Pleroma*,
>
> in his awakening to the Father
> in eternity,
> in his awakening to his brothers
> within time,
>
> in his awakening to his Father
> in every one of his brothers,
> in his awakening to every one of his brothers,
> in the heart of every other being.
>
> In every place the Son awakens to Being.
>
> In every place the Son awakens
> Being springs forth
> between the Father and the Son
> by virtue of their very nature
> in the communion of the Spirit.

---

48. "bosom of the Father": see John 1:18. "In the bosom of the Father . . . awakening in souls" and "In the making of all worlds . . . awakens to Being": variant text of these lines is found as the epigraph for chapter 11, attributed to "Isamuni," in *Sagesse hindoue, mystique chrétienne. Du Védanta à la Trinité* and is translated in *Saccidānanda*.

In the making of all worlds,
in their revolutions,
in the making of humanity,
in all their history,
in their growth,
in the formation of every people
and the unfolding of empires,
in their groping toward the True and the Good,
in the ending of all worlds,
the Son, in the bosom of the Father,
awakens to Being.

Before Time,
since Time began,
within Time
and beyond Time:
where human thought contemplates,
where the mind wavers
in the original silence,
in divine solitude,
in Creation and the Incarnation,
in the Cross and Resurrection,
in the Ascension and the Spirit's Descent,
in every preparation
and every one of the Church's steps,
in humanity's every step toward the Church,
in the Church's fulfillment in Glory,
in the final *Pleroma*,
in the Peace of Eternity,
in consummated Love,
in the Lord's Joy where everyone at last
returns,

the Son in the bosom of the Father
awakens to Being.

In the Bosom of the Father

For there is one reality: the communication of Life between the Father
and the Son, in the unity of the Spirit
in the bosom of Being.

For that alone IS, and whoever IS, is that which IS.

OM

1956
Mauna Mandir, Kumbakonam

Shrī Ramana was Great[49]

And if it wasn't You, O Christ, who made him great, there must be another who can make souls great in the order of the Spirit.

Since it seems to me Shrī Ramana was as great in the scheme of your mystery as many who adorn themselves with your name and call themselves by it.

If it wasn't Your grace, O Christ, that made him great, then there must be another who dispenses grace—some form of grace anyway,

unless one can make himself great without recourse to Your grace or your Spirit, Your grace or anything else.

But then, O Christ, if it is You who made him so great, how will those who bear your sign on their brows in the sight of men not stumble on his greatness when, by chance or grace, they meet him!

For on his brow (which does indeed shine) no one can see the Cross imparting its light to him—

no one, not even himself.

And what anguish there is for your disciples who feel the burning of his fire's glare . . .

For too often the Cross fails to shine from the brows of those it has signed,

and what is the Cross without the Spirit?

It is Your divine play to draw people to Yourself through Shrī Ramana, through Your brilliance shining forth from Shrī Ramana's brow, and no one guesses that it was your own Cross, hidden in the *guhā*, wherefrom those rays sprang up,

drawing the crowds to You, to Your Spirit, by Your Spirit, though he remained unknown and undetectable,

running the risk that among those crowds some, carrying your cross on their brows but grown weary of a sign wherefrom the Spirit fails to shine forth, might be led astray.

If You are *Satya*, Truth, if You are *Sat*, Being,

if You are Life and Light,

then it is You, and it can only be You:

---

49. This poem appears in *La montée au fond du cœur*, 214–17 and is translated in *The Ascent to the Depth of the Heart*, 172–74.

the OM of Truth, Immortality, Light,
resounding in our Upanishads,
the *Shabda-Brahman*
who makes our singers and Rishis tremble,
for You are the Word
coming into the world,
giving to all the Voice, *Vāk*,
of which the Spirit alone possesses complete knowledge—
scientiam habet Vocis—[50]
that is born of the Spirit.

It is You, the Light of Dawn, who makes our Arunāchala blush,
You the *Linga* of Fire we venerate in the Temple
at the foot of the Mountain.
And it is You who, in the various *mūrtis*, deign in a worthy *kenosis*
to make Yourself present to Your worshippers,
seeking You in the guise of the beautiful child Murugan,
worshiping kind Gopāla,
and it is You who then lead everyone to the mystery of Your unique Incarnation in the womb of the Virgin Mary,
just as You led the willful Israelites with endless patience from Horeb to Tabor, Mount Moriah to Golgotha.[51]

You who shine forth in the mystery of the *Guhā*, seen there by our Rishis,

---

50. "*scientiam habet Vocis*": "[the Spirit of the Lord . . .] has knowledge of the voice" (Latin); Wis 1:7.

51. Mount Horeb is the site of Moses's encounter with the burning bush (Exod 3:1), one of the sites claimed for God's presentation of the Ten Commandments to Moses (Deut 4:10 etc.), and the site from which the Israelites set off for Canaan, where Mount Tabor lies (Exod 33:1-6; Deut 1:6-8). Though there is this geographical correspondence, Tabor is not mentioned in the Pentateuch accounts, and so it appears Swāmī Abhishiktānanda is referencing the "typological" movement from the Old Testament's theophanic mountain (where God appears to the Israelites on Mount Horeb) to the New Testament's theophanic mountain (where Jesus is transfigured on Mount Tabor [see Matt 17:1-8; Mark 9:2-8; and Luke 9:28-36]). This is reinforced by the correlation of Mount Moriah (where according to tradition both the sacrifice of Isaac was conducted [Gen 22:2] and Solomon's Temple was constructed [2 Chron 3:1]) and Golgotha (where Jesus was crucified [Matt 27:33; Mark 15:22; Luke 23:33; John 19:17]), as Jesus's sacrifice is traditionally seen as the fulfillment of Isaac's sacrifice (Heb 11:17–19, Tertullian, Pseudo-Barnabas, Hillary, Cyprian, et al.) and the sacrifices of the Temple (e.g. Heb 13:11–12).

they say that first you were revealed as "Hidden," *Guhācara*, *Guhātshara*,
Gūdha,

You the Brahman giving ritual potency to our Vedic mantras,

You the incomparable Brahman shining forth as the "I AM" in the eternal Presence of the Father, in the mystery of my own heart, in the bosom of "I,"

You who empty Yourself even into those mysteries not belonging to Your Church

for those who are not yet able to come into Your Church—

even the troops of Joshua were unable to hear the call of the Beatitudes and to taste the Eucharistic manna—[52]

and yet who long for Your Spirit so much more eagerly in their faith and their love

than Your Fathers did when they entered into Canaan:[53]

for the edification of Your Church,

that her members might finally realize

that to sign the brow with the Holy Cross is not enough.
Rather, the brow thus signed must shine forth and glow
with the Glory of the Living God!

*

* *

O my Beloved, why are you hiding under the guise of Shiva and Arunāchala,

of Shrī Ramana the Rishi and Sadāshiva the Naked wanderer

to give me Your grace?

Is it Your divine play?

You take every form!

---

52. The Book of Joshua recounts how Joshua led the armies of Israel throughout Canaan conquering the inhabitants, thus fulfilling the promise to Abraham (Gen 15:18–21; Deut 1:8) that his descendants would possess the Promised Land. Christ's Beatitudes comprise a prominent part of the Sermon on the Mount (Matt 5:3–12), while there is a shorter list of Beatitudes in Luke's Sermon on the Plain (Luke 6:20–22). The Eucharist is instituted by Christ (Matt 26:26–30; Mark 14:22–24; and Luke 22:14–23) at the Last Supper, which typologically fulfills God's sending of Manna to the Israelites in the desert (Exod 16; John 6:25–59).

53. Canaan is the land promised to Abraham by God (Gen 15:18–21; Deut 1:8) and won and divided amongst Israel's tribes by Joshua in the Book of Joshua.

In the Bosom of the Father

You play with us,
   for You want us to seek You out
   beyond every form!
   No form in the world is not You,
   You who hide Yourself from the ignorant,
who reveal Yourself
to those who know!
You condemned Yourself in the person of Pilate,
flogged Yourself in the Roman soldier.

Your Name—may it be blessed!—is invoked in the *naivedya* of our Temples, in the sacred Flame, since You, You made it when you established Your Memorial. Is it not You, in the depths, from whom they receive nourishment, without knowing what the faithful know, when they receive *prasādam*? And is it not Your Spirit that warms them when they, filled with desire, move their joined hands through the Flame?

You are everywhere in Yourself, and in You everything is, O God, Word, primordial Light, the OM whose echo we utter with our lips. You are in Yourself and within Yourself, in our Temples and in our Churches, in the *mūrtis* kept in the *mandirs* and the icons kept in cathedrals.

You, O *Vāk*, O Word, are the Veda the Brahmin priests utter in their rituals. You are the Rig, You the Sāma, You the Yajur. You are the *Udgītha* and all the others. You are the one offering and the One to whom all is offered. You are in that which is offered. For outside of you, what can be?

You are Shiva the Benevolent One, Dakshināmūrti, the Master of Wisdom, Murugan, the Beautiful God, the Child God, Skanda, the Son, Singhesvara, the One who destroys obstacles, Shanmugan with six faces looking everywhere.

You are Nīlakantha who swallows poison for us that you might obtain the *Amrita*, the drink of immortality. You are Natarāja, the victorious Dancer who tramples on the demon you lay low.

And You play Your love games in the sanctuaries of our Tamil land, whom our holy ones sing.

You are *Anbé* Shiva, Shiva who is Love.

November, 1956
Mauna Mandir, Kumbakonam

Poems on Arunāchala
by Shrī Ramana Maharshi

and Adapted into French
by Swāmī Abhishiktānanda

Author's Note

THE FOLLOWING FIVE PIECES are French adaptations of lyric verses Shrī Ramana Maharshi sang in honor of Arunāchala; the author does not seek to offer a translation. Who could effectively bring into a Western language the images, the rhythm, the evocative charm of Tamil poetry! Besides, he did not know Tamil and had only an English translation, a pale reflection of the original. Yet it happened that everything he read in the text resonated within him so profoundly that the words simply sprang up, as if they were from his own heart, so he could repeat them in his mother tongue. He has held faithfully to the general sense of the verses without forcing himself to translate the intricacies slavishly. His fidelity is of a different order. And those who have read the songs in Tamil and who had the privilege of sitting at the feet of the Maharshi or to meditate at Arunāchala can testify that even where images have been transformed, echoes of [the author's] own experience continue and develop what Shrī Ramana allowed to burst forth from his own experience—the poems here spring up from the same unique source. Translations and commentaries cannot reveal Shrī Ramana accurately. No one will ever know him who will not lose himself in the deepest depths of the Self.

In the Bosom of the Father

In the courts of Chidambaram[1]
the Lord, transported by joy,
dances for his Bride—
who does not move.

Here though, at Arunāchala,
the Mountain of Light,
He performs that dance in all his glory,
the Bride hidden in herself,
fixed in the great closeness of his being,
whom nothing can move.

---

1. These stanzas are based on the first stanza of Shrī Ramana Maharshi's poem commonly titled, "The Necklet of Nine Gems," translated below as "The Crown of Sixteen Diamonds." They appear in *Sagesse hindoue, mystique chrétienne. Du Védanta à la Trinité*, 292 and are translated in *Saccidānanda*, 222.

The Nuptial Garland[2]

Envoi

For my Lord and my King,
Arunāchala,
I will make my wedding garland.

Ganapati, the All Gracious,
bless me with your benign hand,
that my song may be worthy of my Spouse!

Refrain

Arunāchala Shiva, Arunāchala Shiva,
Arunāchala!

1

O Arunāchala
when I've meditated on you in the depths of my heart,
outside of myself, you've uprooted me,
when in the depths of my heart I've seen nothing but you,
Arunāchala!

2

My father was "Charm," my mother "Grace,"
like them, let us be inseparable,
you and me only one, O Arunāchala

---

2. A rendering of Shrī Ramana Maharshi's poem commonly referred to as "The Marital Garland of Letters."

In the Bosom of the Father

3

Coming into my home and enticing me to yours,
why did you keep me a prisoner
in the cave of your heart, O Arunāchala?

4

Was it for your own pleasure
or for my own good that you've enticed me?
If you reject me now,
who will they blame but you, O Arunāchala?

5

Avoid their blame!
Why have you pushed me aside?
How can I remain separated from you now,
O Arunāchala?

6

My fickle mind will leave off error
if only it could find you!
When you chain it, you reveal your charm,
Arunāchala!

7

My agitated mind can search for you,
and so it finds peace,
held captive by the vision of your beauty,
Arunāchala!

8

Now that you've seduced me,
if you don't kiss me,
where is your gallantry, Arunāchala?

9

How can you stay asleep
when you mistreat me, O Arunāchala?

10

Are you not also a mother, Arunāchala?
Then it is your duty
to spread your grace and save me

11

Even when my senses
burst in like thieves
upon my depths,
what should I fear?
Are you not ever within my heart,
O my Lord?

12

OM!
Are you not the One, one without a second?
Who can know you?
Who can embrace and encircle you,
O Arunāchala?

13

Who will ever find you?
You are the eye's pupil,
and with eyes you see, Arunāchala

14

Eye of every eye,
who will ever contemplate you,
O Arunāchala?

15

As a magnet attracts iron,
drawing it in and then keeping it close
without break, O Arunāchala,
so you have drawn me

16

O immovable Mountain,
drowned in a sea of grace,
have mercy on me, I pray

17

Though you are Rock,
you are the Ocean of Mercy:
take pity on me, Arunāchala

18

Fiery jewel,
shooting your flames on every side,
burn through the dross of my heart,
O Arunāchala

19

Shine before me like the Master of grace—
purify me, make me worthy of you,
guide me, O Arunāchala

20

Preserve me from the terrible traps
set by other seducers, Arunāchala:
seduce me, kiss me!

21

Like a beggar, I sit before you,
Arunāchala—you stand unmoved
Tell me now, my Lord:
do not be afraid

22

Even before I ask,
you give yourself, so I say:
betray not your name, O Arunāchala

23

Wondrous and delightful fruits
here in my hands filled with grace
drive me mad with ecstasy,
drunk with the Bliss of your Essence

24

Like the currant
in the palm of my hand, you are there:
satiate me with your delightful flavor,
the flavor of truth, Arunāchala

25

You devour those devoted to you,
Arunāchala—
how can I survive
your embrace?

26

Glorious mountain of Love,
praised by Gautama,[3]
guide me with your gracious glance,
Arunāchala

27

Brilliant sun, engulfing the whole World
in your glittering rays—
your grace and your light have opened
the lotus of my heart, my Lord

28

I long to fall prey to your Love,
take me and devour me whole
that I might find rest,
O Arunāchala

29

I came to feed on you . . .
now you feed on me!
And now there is peace, Arunāchala

30

He strips me of every garment,
leaving me naked;
then he clothed me in his love!

---

3. "Gautama": Gautama Maharshi, one of the seven *maharishis* (the title "maharshi" for Shrī Ramana is an adaptation) of the Vedas, is said to have worshipped at Arunāchala; there is a shrine dedicated to him near the mountain today.

31

Rip, tear apart all that covers me,
leave me there, naked,
and adorn me only in your Love

32

There in the depths of my heart,
peaceful rest, my Lord—
where the ocean of joy surges,
every word is extinguished,
every notion disappears

33

Nothing there but joy
yet no word to say, nothing to feel,
recline in peace, O my Beloved,
down in my depths

34

Leave off afflicting me, deceiving—
let your wondrous Being find me at last,
O Incomparable Consciousness, Arunāchala
Show me your Luminous Face,
O Incomparable Consciousness—Arunāchala!

35

Bring me to knowledge of eternal Life
that I might find that glorious and ancient Wisdom,
be free of the world's illusion

36

If you won't embrace me,
I'll burst into tears, dying of grief,
O Arunāchala

37

In the silence, you said: "Do not speak"
And you remain, dwelling in that silence

38

Happiness is a peaceful rest
we taste when we rest in Being:
beyond language, in truth
there am I established, Arunāchala

39

Not moving, not doing a thing, asleep, happy . . .
I can't say, O Arunāchala!

40

Give me wisdom, I pray,
that my ignorance does not keep me from you,
Arunāchala

41

As the bee watches a flower bud,
waiting for it to open,
so you keep watch over my heart

42

Without knowing what being was, I realized
Being is only "that," Arunāchala

43

Show yourself—
the Only Reality, O Incomparable Happiness
The Real is nothing other than the Self,
isn't that what you want us to Know, Arunāchala?

44

You said, "Look within,
open the eyes of the spirit,"
for there we find you

45

Seeking you alone
in endless being!
. . . a bit of myself
I begin to see

46

What good to be born among men,
if we do not find you,
Arunāchala?

47

With your grace I have gone down
into the depths of your Being,
where only the strong may set out,
stripped of themselves, made pure

48

When I sought refuge in you,
my sole Lord,
you devoured me whole and entire,
you Mountain of light

49

Wondrous treasure of divine grace,
found without search,
ensnare my heart's anguish

50

Treasure of grace—holy, divine—
who let yourself be found without search,
steady my wandering mind, O Mountain of grace

51

Taking up your search
with zeal
I have broken my moorings ...
have mercy on me

52

Boldly pursuing your true Being
my boat was engulfed in the waters—
ah! have mercy on me!

53

Searching with zeal
for your Real Being,
I overcame myself in your grace—
unsurpassable

54

In your love
reach out your grace-filled hand!
without the aid
of your encircling arm

I start to sink,
aware of the loosening
of Love's bonds!

55

You who are Spotless,
come to rest in my heart,
that I might find, at last,
eternal joy!

56

Don't laugh at me as I seek your aid
Adorn me in your grace, then look at me,
O Mountain of Love

57

He smiled,
wrapped me in grace and splendor,
when from a long way off
I moved toward him,
searching for refuge:
the light of his heart
attracting me

58

But when I got close
and rushed toward him
—ah—
he would not bow to me
but stood there, immovable,
fixed in himself . . .
then I saw
He was me

59

From the welcome of his Presence
in myself,
touching his very nature,
I lost all consciousness
of myself

60

Rain on me the sweetness
of your Mercy,
before the fire of your Love
burns me to ashes

61

Shatter the identity keeping me from you,
so there is no longer You and Me!
O, let me taste of this Bliss,
of this joy ever vibrant, ever new

62

Give me wings,
and I will fly more subtle than ether
to reach you, lighter than air!

63

The storms in my mind will cease,
the waves of thought subside,
O, when I reach you!

64

When I fled to you
as refuge for all that I am,

I found you completely naked,
clothed only in the air about you

65

You've given birth
within my petty selfishness
to desire for you;
don't abandon me

66

Don't wait for the fragrance arising from my heart
to dissipate, Arunāchala—
hurry! I've kept it
that you might relish it

67

Like a flower in full bloom
your forceful scent
draws me even to your depths

68

Sinking in your shipwreck,
I will never rest until I've reached
the very bottom of your heart—
'til I am sheltered there!

69

Using the tricks of love to get close to me,
haven't you traded your self for mine,
so robbing me of myself?

70

Now that you've abducted me, I know not
whether I live or have died!
You are a deadly Husband, my Lord

71

Arunāchala,
in your heavenly blindness
you have given all and taken nothing:
O worthy exchange!

72

Remember me! look at me!
        touch me! ripen me!
Make us one, O Arunāchala

73

You've driven me mad for you,
freed me from the madness of the world
Give to me the remedy for all madness

74

I am not afraid
when I run to You—
are you afraid to open Your arms?

75

"Ignorance"? "Wisdom"? what use are these words
when with you there is only one,
Arunāchala?

76

My heart has opened like a flower,
scent it with your pleasing fragrance
and make it clean, my Love!

77

Wed me—I beg you!—
and my heart, so fascinated by the world,
will afterward turn to truth

78

One day I overheard someone say your name . . .
but in fact
You had already seized me, Arunāchala

79

I am a terribly frail reed,
O Arunāchala
Be my support

80

You've put me to sleep, drugged me,
then stolen my understanding—
you've shown me knowledge of Your very Self

81

In that enclosed field
where nothing comes and nothing goes,
show me the heroic deeds of your grace

82

Away from my body, from the world outside,
let me rest forever, delighting
ever in the vision of your Splendor

83

You've given me the medicine of confusion,
Arunāchala—
cure my confusion
that your grace may shine in me

84

You whose "Self" has no "self"—
remedy the madness of those who believe in the "self"

85

My body is the secret chamber,
my heart the nuptial bed—
hear me, kiss me,
Arunāchala

86

You love to unite to yourself
the poor, those destitute of all glory
Arunāchala,
is this not your greatest glory?

87

You've lifted the blindness of ignorance
with the ointment of your grace,
and so I am truly yours

88

Having marked me with your seal,
you withdrew me from the world
Then you showed yourself
dancing in Endless Space

89

O Arunāchala,
is this true silence then—
to continue like a lifeless stone,
without love?

90

Unknown to all, who was it
that turned my head,
then thrilled my soul?

91

Secretly, he's made me drunk—
then what licenses did he not take . . .
Who was that, Arunāchala?

92

Rejoice with me, my Love,
in the fields of Endless Space
where there is no day or night

93

I was the target of your love-darts—
they reached me alive
and you devoured me

94

Did you not call me?
I came,
too bad for you—
now do what you've promised

95

The moment you called me you received me
and, entering me, you gave me life
I lost myself

96

You lured me away from home,
stole into my heart,
brought me gently into your own...
these are your holy ways

97

I've betrayed your secret work,
but don't blame me!
Reveal your work of grace
now, and save me!

98

You who alone
shine in the holy books—
let me understand you

99

Put your hand on my heart,
let me share your Bliss—
I beg you: do not abandon me

100

Like snow in water,
let me melt of love within you
who are Love itself, Arunāchala

101

I but thought of you
and was seized in the trap of your grace—
who can escape the net of your Love?

102

You wait for me like a spider over her prey,
you catch me and feed on me,
Arunāchala

103

Those who love you, whispering your blessed name,
O Arunāchala—I love them too
My divine Lover,
I will be the servant
of your servants

104[4]

105

Shine on
as the blessed Savior
of poor wretches like me,
Arunāchala

---

4. Here the numbering of the typescript is written over with one number forward, bringing the total number of stanzas to one-hundred eight but leaving stanza one-hundred four blank.

106

The holy ones have sung you songs through the ages
to melt lovers' hearts—
will you attend to my poor song?

107

O Mountain of Patience,
bring yourself to listen to these songs of madness
Welcome them as a hymn of joy

108

A — RU — NA
My Beloved Lord,
throw your garland around my shoulders,
and carry this one I braided
for you, O my Lord.

The Crown of Sixteen Diamonds[5]

A — RU — NA
O Being, Consciousness, Bliss!
Are you not the Incomparable Self
and my own self too,
and the meeting of these
in the Unique Absolute?
"You are that."
Achala:
Incomparable Perfection—
O come and adore Arunāchala,
the mountain sparkling like gold
The very act of remembering him
assures Salvation!

2

Those who seek refuge
at the lotus feet
of the Lord of Grace
reigning over Arunāchala,
their souls free from every attachment
to the world, goods, parents,
their hearts made evermore pure
in their unflagging search
for his divine grace:
they have escaped what threatens in the dark
and, in the perpetual light
of his sheltering grace
shining like the dawn,

---

5. Stanzas 1–7 are a rendering of sections from Shrī Ramana Maharshi's poem commonly referred to as "The Necklet of Nine Gems," though the first stanza has been removed, while stanzas 8–16 are a rendering of sections from Shrī Ramana Maharshi's poem commonly referred to as "Eleven Verses to Shrī Arunāchala." Stanzas 1, 9, 12, and 14 appear in *Sagesse hindoue, mystique chrétienne. Du Védanta à la Trinité*, 288–91 and are translated in *Saccidānanda*, 219–22.

they take up their abode in delight,
firm forever
in the Ocean of Bliss!

3

O Arunāchala!
Don't leave me here to languish
for love of you!
Do I not have the memory of you
ever in my heart?
Ah! If I should forget . . .
burn me to ash at once!
Turn your glance toward me,
filled with grace and refreshment,
O Light of my eyes!
Do not abandon me, my Lord,
You who are Incomparable Consciousness,
You whose glory knows no end!
Take up your rest in my heart,
my Lord!

4

O Incomparable Lord,
reigning over Shonagiri,[6]
wondrous Arunāchala:
wipe away my trespasses,
turn your divine Glance toward me,
guide me, generous as the rain of Heaven
Come to my aid,
for I cannot ford the awful torrent
of Total Illusion
without losing myself in this arid waste
You are the Divine Mother of the World—
what could replace the care
a Mother has for her child?

---

6. "Shonagiri": "Red mountain" (Sanskrit); another name for Arunāchala.

5
O Arunāchala!
From the first time you called
all my being was yours!
Who could want anyone else?
You are both
deadly and enlivening!
O center of my life!
Your touch in the depths of my heart
is at once my Death
and my Bliss!

6
Do with me what you will,
my Beloved
Yet grant me only
the grace of melting for love
at your worshipful feet!
To save me
from this wretched human life,
he raised me to Himself,
to gladden his Heart,
that his Presence might break forth,
that the Self might blossom!
Such is my Lord, the Lord of Light,
celebrated throughout the World!

7
In childhood,
you had already revealed Your love for me
in my parents' tender care,
were already hiding there
in my heart!
To prevent my falling
into the deep sea of the World
and drowning,
You drew me forcefully
to Yourself,

holding me prisoner at Your feet,
Arunāchala—
at the very depths of Being,
which You are!

8

You've drawn me to Yourself
by Your grace—
what will become of me
if You don't show me Your Presence?
Do you dare leave me to wander
and lose myself in the darkness of the world,
searching for you without rest
without flagging, with my fervent desire?
O Arunāchala, my Love!
Can the lotus blossom
flourish without light?
You are the Sun's light,
O Spring, pouring forth grace
and letting Your mercy
flow freely!

9

Arunāchala,
the very likeness of grace:
how can you abandon me
now that you've seduced me,
since you see how wretched I am?
Ah! Never let your love
fail to flow in me,
this one who languishes
without respite for love of you!
who longs to melt into You
like wax into fire!
O nectar
pouring forth into the heart
of your Consecrated!
my haven and refuge!

My sole desire is to please you—
there lies all my joy,
Lord of my life!

10

Your Presence
had not even brushed against my consciousness
though you had already begun holding me prisoner
by your grace,
ready to devour me whole and entire
What have I done, wretch that I am,
that you should leave
Your work unfinished?
Why do you torture me,
leaving me suspended
between life and death?
O Arunāchala,
fulfill your intention
and, between the two of us,
leave only yourself,
O Unique Lord!

11

I was struggling there amidst so many
in the surging, stormy waves
belonging to the Ocean of the World
What were you to gain by saving me,
keeping me safe at your feet?
O Lord, you Ocean of grace,
Your very memory routs my confusion
Glory to You, Glory unending!
I bow before You and bless You;
I greet you and thank you!

12

Then you seized me
in secret—
and since that time you've held me prisoner

at your feet, O Lord
When people ask who you are,
I hold silence, head down,
silent as a statue!
Lord, relieve me
in my distress
I'm like a deer in a trap
who kills himself struggling
Lord Arunāchala,
what do you want from me?
But who am I
to try to know your mind?

13
Lord of my life,
here I stand at your feet,
a toad struggling
to climb a lotus stem!
Make me a bee
diving to the flower's heart,
getting drunk on the nectar
of Pure Consciousness—
Then there will be salvation!
If you let me die
as I embrace your worthy feet,
it would be a source of shame for you,
you, the glittering Column of light,
Arunāchala,
the wondrous expanse of grace
scattered everywhere!

14
O Spotless One,
if every living thing
and the five elements,
every manifest thing,
are all merely the splendor
of your all-pervading Light,

how can I then—I alone—
be distinct from You?
Since you shine in the heart,
an endless Expanse that leaves no room
for an "other,"
how, in my own heart,
can I come forth distinct from you?
Come forth alone in my heart
and root your lotus feet
on the head of my "I"
even as it strives to assert itself

15

Even from my youth you kept me
from knowledge discerned in human reason,
rooting me in Abiding Peace
Ah! Happy chance!
for the death of the self is a blessing
that leads to Truth!
O Incomparable God,
you appeared
as a mountain of light
to illumine the world and save it
from evil,
to save me, poor and wretched—
though mad for love of you
Grant me the awesome grace
of embracing your worthy feet!

16

O Transcendent One:
look at my poverty,
how much I yet fail
to reach your Incomparable Wisdom,
finally free from all attachment
Destroy my liberty, I beg you!
Let me place my burden
in your arms,

In the Bosom of the Father

for what could weigh down the heart
of the one who supports the World?
O my God,
Incomparable Lord,
I've suffered too much
to bear this earthly life alone,
without your help, O Arunāchala!
You are Being, the Self!
I can no longer live
apart from You
Leave off, I beg you!
don't let me languish
far from you!

Nine Gems[7]

I found a new thing. This mountain is a magnet. It holds firm anyone who even thinks of it, drawing him face-to-face with it, rendering him as still as itself and devouring him. Hear this, and live. Know that this kidnapper is the magnificent Arunāchala, shining within the heart!

How many hearts have already been ravaged by only thinking of this mountain, the Incomparable One? Friends, you who are disgusted with this life, weary in body, there is on the earth a wondrous drug that, without killing one, annihilates anyone who simply recalls it: none other than Arunāchala.

Listen: it looks like a mountain, lacking consciousness and feeling. Its action is mysterious, surpassing all human understanding. Even in my childhood, it shone within my dreams as something of incomparable greatness. And still I can't understand it. Then it drew me in, silenced my thoughts—I came close and found that it was complete stillness.

"Who is it who sees?" When I descended to search for him in the depths, he was no longer there. No thought came to me saying "I have seen"—so how could the thought "I have not seen" arise? Who could convey this in words, when even You Yourself could not gesture toward it in ancient days except through silence? And You alone reveal in the midst of Silence that You remain here in the form of this Mountain, pouring out light from the heavens to the earth.

When I approach You and gaze upon You, You appear in the form of an earthly mountain. But when I consider you as Formless, then I pass from earth to the ether. When I dwell on your nature, forsaking thought, do I not lose my own identity, just as a bit of sugar does when it is dissolved in water? When I come to realize that I am, what happens to "me"?

To seek God and ignore You, You who are pure Being, pure Consciousness—is this not using a lamp to search out darkness? It is only to make yourself known as pure Being and pure Consciousness that you permit

---

7. This first two stanzas of this poem rendered in prose are a free rendering of stanzas from Shrī Ramana Maharshi's poem commonly known as "Eleven Verses to Shrī Arunāchala," while the remaining stanzas are a free rendering of stanzas from Shrī Ramana Mahrshi's poem commonly known as "Eight Stanzas to Shrī Arunāchala." They appear in *Sagesse hindoue, mystique chrétienne. Du Védanta à la Trinité*, 285–87 and are translated in *Saccidānanda*, 216–18.

yourself to be called by so many names and loved in so many forms. Truly, those who fail to know you are like the blind, who do not know the Sun—O Arunāchala the Great, the Jewel without peer. Abide here and shine as my own Self, You, the One without a second!

Like a string threaded through gems, you penetrate the great diversity of beings. You are the wheel upon which the mind is freed from its flaws, like the precious stone the jeweler cuts and polishes. But is it not enough for the mind to touch you for it to take on the brilliance of your grace, to shine like a ruby that cannot be darkened? Can a photosensitive plate once exposed to the sun take on any other image? O Arunāchala, Mountain of grace and glory, is there anything aside from You?

When the thought "I" vanishes, is there a place for any other thought? In the past when thoughts arose in consciousness, there was the question "Who thinks these things?" and the response came back, "It is me." But the one who continues the inquiry, searching for the source of this "I," diving within—that one reaches the heart and passes over to the incomparable Lord. You Ocean of grace and splendor, shoreless, O Arunāchala, dancing in stillness in the courts of my heart! Where then are these pairs of words: within and without, birth and death, pleasure and pain, light and dark?

The waters rise from the sea in the form of clouds; they plunge back to the earth in rain, becoming streams that return to the sea. Nothing can prevent them from returning to their source. How could the soul that springs from You be prevented from returning to You? A bird leaves the earth flying, floats through the air, but she has no place to rest: she must return to the earth. Just so, one must return in one's own way, and when the soul finally finds its way back to its source, it will immerse and sink itself into you, O Arunāchala, Ocean of Bliss.

=

Five Rubies[8]

1

O Ocean of nectar,
Vast Store of grace—
the whole World
is engulfed in your splendor,
Arunāchala!
Incomparable Self,
in your brilliant Fullness
the lotus of my heart
opens to Bliss

2

O Arunāchala!
You created the world,
in you it endures,
in You it is dissolved—
a Wonder!
You are the inner Self
who dances in the courts of my heart,
more myself than I am—
You are called "the Heart"

3

Whoever dives
into the depths
of his silent soul
to the well-spring
of his ego,
that one realizes the "self"
and is lost in You,

---

8. This poem is a rendering of Shrī Ramana Maharshi's poem commonly referred to as "Five Stanzas to Shrī Arunāchala." It appears in *Sagesse hindoue, mystique chrétienne. Du Védanta à la Trinité*, 288–89 and is translated in *Saccidānanda*, 219–20.

O Arunāchala,
like a wave
in the sea!

4
Withdrawn from the world,
the heart and senses calmed,
the ascetic contemplates you
in the very depths of his heart,
O Arunāchala!
Your light illumines
his heart,
and he finds in You
his own Fullness

5
Whoever consecrates body and soul
to You,
contemplating the world
as a reflection of your grace,
worshipping You and loving You
as the Incomparable Self—
that one loses himself in You,
O Arunāchala,
Ocean of happiness!

Poems on Arunāchala by Shrī Ramana Maharshi

Author's Note: The following four pieces are [the author's] French adaptations of didactic poems by Shrī Ramana Maharshi.

Ulladu Narpadu I[9]

If there were no being,
who would there be to think of being?
and if there were no self,
who would there be to have consciousness?
who would there be to say "I"
at the source of thought,
at the very depths of the self,
deeper than thought,
closer than the self,
the inner mystery of everything,
the mystery of being,
the mystery of the ego?
Who will ever find this,
save the one alone turned within himself,
his thought lacking thought,
lacking a self to say "I"—
become himself at last?

---

9. This stanza is a very free rendering of the first stanza of Shrī Ramana Maharshi's poem commonly referred to as "Reality in Forty Verses," given by Shrī Ramana to the Tamil poet Shrī Muruganar who had asked the Maharshi for a cycle of verses that would give a summary of the master's teaching.

Shrī Ramana Gītā II.2[10]

Within the depths,
in the deepest hollows of the cave of the heart,
the incomparable I, the Incomparable SELF
unique and alone,
Brahman shines.
With spirit and senses calmed,
the mind at rest in itself,
fathom and sink into what lies within
at Your deepest depths,
ever fixed in the SELF.

---

10. This stanza is a rendering of chapter II, verse 2 of the *Shrī Ramana Gītā*, composed by the Maharshi's disciple, Shrī Kavyakantha Ganapati Muni, based on discussions conducted mostly in 1916–1917.

Praise in Truth[11]

1

Give glory to the Lord
from a heart that does not seek its own—
    thus will you purify your mind
and reach Salvation

2

Your body praises the Lord when you prostrate before his Face
Your voice praises the Lord when you chant him hymns
Your thoughts praise the Lord when you meditate on his name:
    step by step
    toward the goal

3

Think on the Lord as Master of the World,
    worship him in the eight forms[12]—
        a holy act

4

But within the praise uttered with your lips
    don't forget
the silent prayer springing up from the heart

5

Like oil spreading or a river ceaseless in its flowing,
so your thought must ever cling to the Lord

---

11. This poem is a very free rendering of verses 3–10 of Shrī Ramana Maharshi's poem commonly referred to as "The Essence of Instruction" ("Upadesha Sāram").

12. "eight forms": the world, comprised of the five elements, the sun, the moon, and the individual being.

6

But greater than thought fixed on Him
    is the thought
that you are not other than Him

7

    And greater than this last:
when there is nothing left that thinks or is thought—
    this is Praise in Truth

8

When the mind is fixed in the heart,
    come back to its source.
    Then all paths of yoga are brought together—
of works, of devotion, of knowledge[13]

---

13. "of works ... of knowledge": three paths of yoga: Karma Yoga, Bhakti Yoga, Jnāna Yoga.

The Way of Being[14]

1

Remove your mind
from what your senses grasp,
and contemplate within
your own form as light:
thus will you see the vision of being

2

Plunge into thought until you find its bottom—
once that fades away,
there is the true way of being

3

Look: the mind is nothing but thought,
and the foundation of every thought is that of the self—
is there anything else to the mind
aside from this thought of the self?

4

This "I" in every thought you think—
search out where it springs forth
and you will only see him escape

5

At the same moment it vanishes,
in the depths
the true *AHAM* appears

---

14. This poem is a very free rendering of verses 16–30 of Shrī Ramana Maharshi's poem commonly referred to as "The Essence of Instruction" ("Upadesha Sāram"). It appears in *Sagesse hindoue, mystique chrétienne. Du Védanta à la Trinité*, 283–84 and is translated in *Saccidānanda*, 215–16.

6
When you lie in deep sleep,
what "I" can your thought utter then?
And yet You are

7
Body, sense, breath, thought—
all this is but darkness, lifeless, not "being"
You are, you, neither this nor that:
You are

8
Consider this: the one who knows what is—
can he be someone else?
Being, consciousness of self:
You are That![15]

9
The divine Self and you, in truth you are that
Being is one
Only in the mind does thought produce differentiation

10
Among all people, the one who realizes that he is,
in the absolute,
he alone has the vision of the self—
in this vision is the vision of God

11
To know the self is to remain fixed in the self:
can the self be another?
The self is being

---

15. "You are That": *tat tvam asi* (Sanskrit); Chāndogya Upanishad 6.8.7; one of the *mahāvākya*s ("great sayings") from the Upanishads.

12
Beyond knowing and not-knowing
alone is true knowledge—
there where nothing remains to be known

13
When one reaches true knowledge of the self,
there is nothing but being
without beginning or end,
the endless joy of the consciousness of being

14
There never were bonds,
never salvation
Realize this: You are That

15
There never was ignorance,
never any knowledge to gain:
forevermore You are

16
You who realize this are the perfect devotee,
you who realize this are the perfect ascetic:
so says Shrī Ramana, the very Consciousness of Self

Poems from the Diary
of Swāmī Abhishiktānanda

Translator's Note: The following poems are found in Swāmī Abhishiktānanda's journal from April 1952 through July 1973. While we are not sure Swāmī Abhishiktānanda thought of these as pieces for possible publication, they are lineated, dwell on similar themes as his poems prepared for publication, and employ many of the same images, tropes, and schemes as those prepared for publication.

IN THE BOSOM OF THE FATHER

In silence you taught me silence

In silence you taught me silence,
O Arunāchala—
you who never leave your silence.

April 4, 1952
Vanatti Cave, Arunāchala

Poems from the Diary of Swāmī Abhishiktānanda

O Arunāchala

O Arunāchala—
Shiva, benevolent and gracious,
Shānta, peaceful,
Advaita, One without a second,
Pūrna, fullness,
Ānanda, bliss—
you didn't stop until you brought me
to your lotus feet,
forcing me to enter the cave of your heart.
How much and how long
have you ravished my heart like this?
A moth, I've let you trick me into your flame,
and you consumed me.
Consume me, burn in me all that isn't You.
O Column of Fire, O Column of Love,
O *Tejo-Linga*, O Sperm of Fire,[1]
from your Fire let me be reborn as You!
Once I thought I had left everything,
and a second time as well—
your irresistible call has shown me
what it means to leave all for You;
until that day I hadn't left anything.
Keep me at your lotus feet,
keep me in the crypt of your heart.
This world that I have left once,
twice, finally, and for good for You,
erase it from my very being,
that I might remain in You Yourself
naked, alone, with no words.
In silence you taught me silence,

---

1. In one variant of the story of Skanda's birth, Shiva's sperm generates his son (the place of his conception varies in different accounts), but only after he ejaculates in spite of himself and the god of fire, Agni, receives the seed. Unable to consume it, Agni deposits it in the River Ganges.

In the Bosom of the Father

O Arunāchala—
You who never leave your silence.
Don't let me enter Your cave in vain,
let nothing remain of "me" and "mine."
Let me pass into you, let me become You—
not "In You Yourself,"
for that no longer satisfies.
To say "You" is to say "I,"
and you have burned up even the traces of "I."
Your "I" alone continues, O incomparable Self.
In You I say *Brahma aham asmi*[2]
and I am absorbed.[3]

*
* *

Long has your whisper called me,
making me cross the seas,
and, entering Your Bosom, I have found a peace
I had never felt,
peace, fullness, joy—
shānti, pūrnam, ānandam.
But your peace is not enough,
your joy is not enough.
If I feel peace, if I feel joy,
then I haven't reached the final depths,
where alone and without a second, *advaita,* You are.
You shine in the form of the Self.
You are "I."
I seek forgetfulness of everything,
only the memory of You,
Your own eternal consciousness
in a peace, a joy too pure
to be felt as mine, in what is alone essential.

---

2. "*Brahma aham asmi*": "I am Brahman" (Sanskrit); Brihadāranyaka Upanishad 1.4.10; one of the *mahāvākyas* ("great sayings") from the Upanishads.

3. "In silence … am absorbed": excerpted for *The Secret of Arunāchala* (1979), 28 n. 5.

Poems from the Diary of Swāmī Abhishiktānanda

*
* *

The Lord has chosen places where his grace is more strongly felt, where his
    love pours out more abundantly.
He prepared them with zeal from the foundations of the earth,
    and established the mountains above the abyss.[4]
The sages have found them and hidden within,
    to be flooded with Your Light, set ablaze in Your Fire.
—In those places people have sensed You,
translating You into myths.
—Column of Fire, Column of Love,
Home of the "Spirit"!
In Your sacred Heart I've taken refuge,
in the cave on your side,
where I am reborn from Water and Fire.
—O Jesus, resplendent Dawn, red with your Blood
and your Love, *Aruna*—Mountain of the Dawn, Arunāchala!
Jesus the Advaita, the Only Son of the Father,
to whom we are not second
but in whom we are all the Only Son,
and in whose Spirit we are all One with the Father:
Jesus who is Grace, Jesus who is Peace,
Jesus Brahman!

April 6, 1952
Vanatti Cave, Arunāchala

---

4. "He prepared ... the abyss": cf. Prov 8:23, 25.

I am not this

I am not this.
I am below this or above this.
I am its source.
I shouldn't—couldn't—have anxiety or desire concerning this.
I am not this. I am deeper in the depths.
I am immersed in the source's depths.
Below this at its center, feeling nothing, I see all in peace.
I shouldn't allow any sound. I want to break these depths and enter inside.
Reach *sat cit ānanda*, immersed in them, realizing my real I.
I am further, below, deeper than the self that speaks, eats, looks, listens, walks, thinks, desires.
When I sleep, I have no desire, no thought, I do not move.
And yet, I am.
I can break the stronghold of this body and seek my real home.
Though I say "my real home," it is not a home. *Aham* has no body, no name.
In breaking that stronghold of the body and entering within, I am beyond place and time.
In saying "here," there is no place.
In saying "now," there is no time.
I praise my *ahamtvam*.
The Holy Spirit teaches some to perform wonders, others to speak in tongues, others to teach, and more besides.[5] To those whom he has given the grace, he shows the way of *ahamtvam*. The Father and I are one.[6]
Even if I don't live the life of a *sannyāsī* completely, I am a *sannyāsī*.
Sannyāsa without the Spirit is a body without life.[7] It has the appearance without, a false appearance. Such a lifeless *sannyāsī* can put on the saffron robe, eat food he's received as alms, live alone and in silence. All these are external signs. They follow observances with difficulty.

---

5. "The Holy . . . to teach": cf. 1 Cor 12:8–10.

6. "The Father . . . are one": John 10:30.

7. There seems to be an error in the French edition of the diary here, where "dans l'Esprit" (apparently) should be "sans l'Esprit." The English translation of the diary adopts this emended reading.

Poems from the Diary of Swāmī Abhishiktānanda

For a false *sannyāsī* silence is difficult.
For a true *sannyāsī*, speaking is difficult—it is an aggravation.

June 3, 1952
Vanatti Cave, Arunāchala
Originally in Tamil

Offer this moment as an Offering

Offer this moment as an Offering and receive the gift of this moment. The gift to me of this moment is truly nothing but the gift to the Son of the eternity rising up from the bosom of the Father.

To accept it is to offer it.

To know it, to rejoice in the Bliss of the Spirit.

To accept it: faith; to know it, to rejoice in it: to love with the love of the Spirit.

It is to be fulfilled, to let oneself be fulfilled in the Spirit's indrawn breath, and to be fulfilled in the Spirit is to fulfill God—

God, who cannot be fulfilled within himself in eternity, in his Spirit, without us being fulfilled in this moment, in his Spirit.

For my moment is God's eternity.

Hear the laughter of people, of birds, hear their love and their songs—in the present moment that passes, abide in the eternity that abides.

Like a child playing in the moments that succeed one another, like a child playing in the eternity that abides—

in that play he draws me in, and if I resist being drawn into his game,

if I play the sulking child who says, "I don't want to play! No way!" then from Eternity I fall into time,

from Spirit to the flesh.

I eat the apple, the fruit of the Tree of Knowledge

I know how to choose between good and evil

I know how—rather, I think I know how—to decide for myself, how I would decide for God.

June 8, 1952
Vanatti Cave, Arunāchala

This life in the Depths[8]

This life in the Depths—the *guhā*—where alone with God I am.
This life in the Depths, where alone in God I am.
This life in the Depths, where alone from God I am.
This life in the Depths, where alone is the One who is . . .
"With God" is the creature's plane.
"In God" is the Spirit's plane.
"From God" is the Son's plane.
"Where alone is the One who is" is the Father's plane—
    the final ascent within unity, within Deity.

April 12, 1953
Shāntivanam

---

8. This poem appears in *Souvenirs d'Arunâchala* (1978), 80 n. 15 and is translated in *The Secret of Arunâchala* (1979), 54 n. 9.

Discover at the center of the self

Discover at the center of the self the source of the self.
Discover in the source of the self, the Self in its source.
Discover the source in the self of the Self in its source.

December 5, 1953
Cave of Arutpāl Tīrtha, Arunāchala

Within the depths

Within the depths,
in the incomparable darkness,
a single flame springs forth.
Who can tell the flame's secret?
the mystery of One?
the mystery of Three?
He alone knows it
but will never repeat it,
who has fallen into the flame,
consumed in it,
passed into the flame,
become One.

> December 10–20, 1953
> Cave of Arutpāl Tīrtha, Arunāchala

Beyond the Depths

Beyond the Depths,
within the Darkness,
beyond the OM,
within the "heart of Arunāchala,"
beyond all manifestation—
the silence of *avyakta*.
Who can tell silence's secret,
the mystery of One,
the mystery of Three,
the mystery of the Word,
the mystery of *AHAM*,
the mystery of the OM?
He alone knows
but will never repeat it,
who has dived into the silence
and become that same silence.

December 21, 1953
Cave of Arutpāl Tīrtha, Arunāchala

Departure from Arunāchala

Night. What was singing in me—within my depths, in the heart of Arunāchala, while the train carried my body away from Arunāchala:

Why do you let me leave, O Arunāchala?

To others, you say: "Va, va."[9]

Why then do you say to me, "Gun, gun"?[10]

Why did you draw me to your lotus feet but not leave me there, prostrate, forever?

Why did you draw me into the heart of your heart but not leave me hidden there, forgotten?

Why did you draw me to your summit, into your flame, but not leave me there, consumed?

It would be so easy for you to keep me there with you, no longer willing to hear any call from without.

Every time I come to you, there is a new birth,

every day beside you is like a year's life,

but every time you end up sending me back to rejoice or to weep in a *svarga* far from you.

Will one more time be the last? the one from which there's no coming back—*na punar āvartate*?[11]

Then you'll have made me pass so deeply into yourself that no call will ever draw me out.

They will call. They might even command.

But there will no longer be anyone to be called, to be commanded.

This "me" they were accustomed to addressing will be no more,

for there will then be only you.

And when they call me, there will be no one to respond,

sunk as I will be in You,

in the flame of your heart,

become your inmost "Self"

in becoming my inmost "self"

9. "Va, va": "Come, come" (Tamil).
10. "Gun, gun": "Go, go" (Tamil).
11. "*na punar āvartate*": "he does not return" (Sanskrit); Chāndogya Upanishad 8.15.1.

in the flame on your summit,
passed into that flame and become You in it,
in becoming myself,
becoming your summit—
at once the deepest hollow and the highest peak
of Arunāchala,
fulfilling in myself the *vyakta* of Arunāchala.
At the inmost point of his being,
at the deepest point of his source,
at the highest point of his eternal springing up,
only becoming myself in this *avyakta*
itself
of Arunāchala
in the center of the heart,
from which nothing yet has sprung forth
in the flame on his summit,
once the springing forth has ceased.

December 27, 1953
On a train departing from Arunāchala

POEMS FROM THE DIARY OF SWĀMĪ ABHISHIKTĀNANDA

Renounce my *God*

Renounce *my* God, which isn't renouncing God.
Renounce *my* joy, which isn't renouncing joy.
Renounce *my* peace, which isn't renouncing peace.
Renounce my renunciation.

March 8, 1956
Tirukoyilūr

Seek God until you find him beyond

Seek God until you find him beyond every thought, every feeling of him,
   beyond your thoughts on his unthinkability,
   beyond your feelings about the inability to experience him.
   And to seek God, seek also yourself,
   beyond the subject of whom you are aware that "he perceives," "he feels," "he thinks,"
   beyond the subject who is aware that "he perceives himself," "he feels himself," "he thinks of himself."
   As long as you remain aware of yourself, you have not reached yourself.
   You are as far from yourself as God is.
   God is as close to you as you are.
   God is as far from you within yourself as he is outside of yourself.
   Travel the starry firmament, out beyond the galaxies, and still you will not have reached God. God's heaven is beyond all the heavens we can reach by reason or sense.
   The mystery you bear within yourself is itself beyond all the galaxies your mind can explore.
   God is as transcendent to you when you look upon him within as when you look upon him without.
   And equally inaccessible.
   And you yourself are as inaccessible to yourself as God within you is inaccessible to you,
   for your own mystery is itself the mystery of God.
   And it is a mystery of God even deeper than the mystery of God in himself—poor reason stammers!
   The divine immanence lies at the furthest borders of Transcendence. And the *apara brahman*, the immanent, is in truth reached at the very heart of *para brahman*.

June 14, 1956
Shāntivanam

If I am, how can You be?

—If I am, how can You be?
    You, my brother, my friend, the unknown, my God?
—If I were not, how could You be?

November 6, 1956
Mauna Mandir, Kumbakonam
On the banks of the Kāverī
At the beginning of the 32-day silent retreat

The awakening to Jesus's being

The awakening to Jesus's being—*Deus dixit ad me*...[12]
The awakening to Buddha Gautama's being—*OM mani padme hum*...[13]
The awakening to the *rishi*'s being—*OM tat sat*...*OM*...[14]
The awakening to the being of all beings in the one who awakens to the being of all his being

abhinna, undivided, *akhanda, asparsha*.
Everything is a *mūrti* of being. What does the particular *mūrti* matter?

November 8, 1956
Kumbakonam

---

12. "*Deus dixit ad me*": "God said to me" (Latin); Ps 2:7.

13. "*Om mani padme hum*": often translated as "Om the jewel in the lotus Hum" with the first and last syllables being mantra syllables without particular semantic meaning (Sanskrit).

14. "*OM tat sat*": "Om, That (is) the (absolute) Being or Real" (Sanskrit); one of the *mahāvākyas*; see Shvetāshvatara Upanishad 1.16 and *Bhagavad Gītā* 17.23.

I will sing a song for my beloved

I will sing a song for my Beloved,[15]
my Lord Arunāchala,
with words he himself drew from my heart
in his own heart.
I will weave a garland of flowers
for my Beloved, Shiva Arunāchala,
flowers he himself picked in the garden of my heart
in his own heart.
I will thread pearls
to adorn Your neck, my Beloved,
pearls that, diving down, You Yourself found
in the ocean of my heart,
in the depths of Your heart.
I will mix balm for You,
for Your ebony hair, my Beloved,
adorned by the crescent moon
with the choicest perfumes You Yourself have distilled
in the corolla of my heart
in the depths of Your heart.
And I will sprinkle purifying water on Your Feet,
O my Beloved,
which You Yourself have made to spring up
in the greatest depths of my heart
in Your own heart.
And I will wave the blazing flame before You
that You Yourself lit in my bosom
at Arunāchala
in Your depths.
And I will burn myself like incense
I offer before You,
which has come from You and goes to You,
nothing but You Alone,

15. "I will sing . . . my beloved": cf. Isa 5:1, "Cantabo dilecto meo canticum" ("I will sing a song to my beloved").

In the Bosom of the Father

O Arunāchala.
And I have ashes too, pure white ashes
to sign Your forehead and Your breast,
Your shoulders and Your arms,
with the three mystical lines.
Ashes, my Arunāchala,
leftover from my heart
where You've burned
like a devouring flame,
O Arunāchala!

November 11, 1956
Kumbakonam

I came here to make you known

I came here to make You known to my Hindu brothers,
but it is You who have made Yourself known to me in them,
in the overwhelming features of Arunāchala!

November 14, 1956
Kumbakonam

The mystery I carry within

The mystery I carry within—how can it be two? At times it is called Jesus, at times Arunāchala.
It seems you laugh at my anguish,
playing a cruel game of hide-and-seek with me,
O Jesus Arunāchala!

November 15, 1956
Kumbakonam

In serene solitude, in sovereign solitude

In serene solitude, in sovereign solitude.
In serene fullness, in sovereign fullness.
In bliss,
in the solitude of my fullness,
in the fullness of my solitude,
in the solitude of my bliss,
in the bliss of my solitude.
Alone, with nothing in the firmament or on earth.
The agony of Jesus at Gethsemane and Calvary—
Deus, Deus meus ut quid dereliquisti me?[16]
At the center of the *guhā*, the triple mystery,
not more one than another,
because *asparsha*.
Snatched up by being,
the *spiritus* snatched up by the *Spiritus* within.

November 17, 1956
Kumbakonam

---

16. "*Deus, Deus . . . dereliquisti me*": "My God, my God, why have you abandoned me?" (Latin); Ps 22:2; Matt 27:46; Mark 15:34.

But when Christ came to earth

But when Christ came to earth, he was God without intermediary. But how often do people still stop at the "sacrament" which was Christ's body? "It is better for you that I leave, for if I do not go away" how else would you receive the Spirit?[17]

People were afraid—penetrating to the depths of their hearts, face-to-face with themselves, to the depths of the heart of Christ—to meet the Father face-to-face, the living God,
> at the wellspring of life itself,
> of the life beyond every veil, beyond every sign,
> in the reality of him "who is."

Yet Jesus said to Nicodemus: "You must be reborn in the Spirit."[18] The Kingdom of God can only be reached by returning to your mother's womb, in the baptism in the great waters of the beginning.
> *mama yonih apsvantah samudre*
> *ya evam veda sa devīpadam āpnoti*
> *aham suve pitaram asya mūrdhan*[19]

. . .

The one called by grace, and by his own love also, to be what he is eternally in the love of the Father, of which he is born in the Spirit,
> in the waters and the fires of the Spirit,
> in his overwhelming waters,
> in his devouring flames,
> in his breath that carries one off:
> where has he gone, the one who tried to get there?
> where has he gone, the one who was carried off?
> How could he even know?

---

17. "It is . . . go away": John 17:7.
18. "You must . . . the Spirit": see John 3:3–8.
19. *"mama yonih . . . asya mūrdhan"*: "My womb is in the waters, in the ocean; the one who knows this reaches the place of the goddess. I have given birth to the Father on the summit" (Sanskrit); see Devī Upanishad 7 and Rig Veda 10.125.7.

Christian thought has admirably firmed up these archetypal intuitions of human consciousness as it received them from the unique experience of Jesus, the Christ, the Word, the only Son of the Father, co-eternal and consubstantial,

from whom proceeds the Spirit, God "resting" upon the world, upon the Servant, upon the Son, the Spirit who is the mystery of the Father-in-the-Son.

And the Church in her sacrament returns humanity back to its origins—"no one, unless he is reborn," *nisi quis renatus fuerit*—bringing it to fulfillment.[20]

To the Father by the Spirit.

It is precisely this that makes humanity a race apart—that it can be reborn in the Spirit.

You will be saved, says St. Paul, if you confess with the lips that Jesus is Lord, and if you believe in your heart that he rose from the dead.[21]

That is, you have awoken to being in Jesus,
within Being, the Father,
and in Jesus you have reached Lordship of the world,
sarveshvara sarvajna . . .
and you are
and the world is in you
in that depth of the self
where there is nothing but You,
the You of Jesus to the Father, in Being.

Being reborn in the primordial origins, beyond one's human birth and one's cosmic birth, going beyond and before those myths, like that of Hindu *samsāra*, in which humanity tries to live with its basic incapacity for being . . . beyond that basic inadequacy, as inaccessible to my reason as to my consciousness

rebirth in awakening to being, in one's first awakening,
in the first awakening
beyond death, final death.
When nothing remains, nothing at all,
not even rest in God's love for oneself.
Eli, eli lamma sabacthani?[22]

---

20. "no one . . . *renatus fuerit*": John 3:5.
21. "You will . . . the dead": Rom 10:9.
22. "*Eli, eli lamma sabacthani*": "My God, my God, why have you forsaken me?"

The Resurrection.

(Paul applies the *Filius meus es tu* to the Resurrection of Jesus.[23] Christmas is a feast that came later into the liturgy as into Christian consciousness.)

The rebirth,

before which, indeed, there was no birth,

since it is

before all eternity.

No awakening to being in the depths of the self is not at the same time an awakening to being in every being, and in all the history of the world and humanity, in the history of each person, in all one's own history.

The yogic return to the self is not fruitful in itself, but only then does it have a result. Understand it like this:

ayam ātma brahman...[24]

Be what you are, just this: *ātmanishtha tvam bhava*.[25]

November 30, 1956
Kumbakonam

("Eli, eli," Hebrew; "lamma sabacthani," Aramaic); Ps 22:2; Matt 27:46.

23. "*Filius meus es tu*": "You are my Son" (Latin);); Ps 2:7; Mark 1:11; Luke 3:22; Acts 13:33.

24. "*ayam ātma brahman*": "this Self is Brahman" (Sanskrit); Māndūkya Upanishad 1.2; one of the *mahāvākyas* ("great sayings") from the Upanishads.

25. "*ātmanishtha tvam bhava*": "stay established in the ātman" (Sanskrit); cf. the last line of *Shrī Ramana Gītā* II.2.

Advaita is when one has plunged into the guhā

Advaita is when one has plunged into the *guhā*,
has sunk
into the bosom of the Father.
Then, everything looks different, for nothing then appears any different,
and it is a taste that overwhelms every other taste, an entirely different taste, and yet no taste is any different from it.
But this is a teaching that will not fight other doctrines.
It simply is.
In sinu Patris.[26]

December 1, 1956
Kumbakonam

---

26. *"In sinu Patris"*: "in the bosom of the Father" (Latin); John 1:18.

In this darkness

In this darkness, sometimes a glimmer presages the sun, a firefly fluttering about the *ākāsha* of my heart.

Yet it is still true that some help us to find that place, gurus who help us to meet the guru, books that help us hear the voice, sacraments that help us enter into the mystery:

this place, which is not a place in space, this guru who has no form, this voice that has no sound, that does not resound in space, this mystery no symbol can express.

This place in myself where being originates (in human terms),

this place in myself where my "I am" originates,

this place in myself where the thought that "I am" originates.[27]

All the same, one day I will finally come to where I understand that I am, where I no longer play with this thought and this extraordinary consciousness that I am, without taking into account what it contains within itself, where I seize its truth. And then it will explode in my poor *manas*, unable to bear such power, and my ego, my *manas*, my *buddhi*, all that will burst too. Liberating the primordial energy—whose most adequate symbol is now the atomic explosion, though still inadequate. For when the atom explodes it becomes another atom, while when the ego explodes it remains, completely, integrally itself, and yet it knows thereafter where it is . . .

The *advaitin* is the one who does not amuse himself with, doesn't play with, doesn't joke about, the "I am."

This explosion of the "I am"—which happened one day in Shrī Ramana, without outward *samādhi*—

this is the appearance of Dakshināmūrti.

December 5, 1956
Kumbakonam

---

27. The French diary has a repetition of the line, "This place in myself where being originates (in human terms)" here, while the (later) English diary has a line similar to the one I translate here.

If I want something

If I want something—even realization—I want only the object of my thought.

The Real is not to be wanted.

It is.

As long as I have not realized that I am, I want anything in vain, for being is not to be wanted. Everything I do is in vain, for being is not to be done.

There is nothing to want, to desire, to seek, to reach.

The solitude of being (of *aham asmi*).[28]

For all that is desired, sought, and reached is human work, human thought—all performed by one-who-is-not-that-which-is.

The past is thought, the future is thought, neither is what is. Be free of the past—the long distant and what was just here. Be free of the future—what will come much later and what will soon be. This is not to say that you should reject your concerns, desires, and regrets with yet another thought just as vain, but quite simply, "to be," to realize directly that I am: *aham asmi*. Nothing more to desire or ask for, nothing to regret, nothing to get, nothing to abandon. *Kevala*.

April 8, 1957
Singhad

---

28. "*aham asmi*": "I am" (Sanskrit); cf. Brihadāranyaka Upanishad 1.4.10; part of one of the *mahāvākyas* ("great sayings") from the Upanishads, the full saying being "*Aham Brahmāsmi*" ("I am Brahman").

Everything is his mūrti

Everything is his *mūrti*, everything is his *linga*, that alone. Meher Baba refused to give his *darshan*.[29] I gain as much in the *darshan* of the laborer carrying my bag as I would from Meher Baba's. And as much when I see the most deprived beggar, an insect, a buffalo, and the most unclean animal. What a burst of laughter, like Claudel's: that *avatāra* as a "pig."[30] No need to give him a Sanskrit name—it was actually in this animal that wallows in the mud and eats excrement that he desired to appear. This is the official teaching of the Doctors of the Law.

He is in the unclean act, and in the act that—to human eyes—appears sublime. Not that he's just there—he's precisely the act itself.

The wagon that passes by, the crates workers move about on the platform, these are precisely the mystery of God.

And people say, "the mystery," to give themselves time to reflect and to preserve the rights of "their" wisdom.

This is the mystery that flows, that flows through things, and people, and other beings, and animals,

that is made, that is unmade, that grows, that continues, that becomes. This is what "is."

All this is the *linga*. This is the *linga*.

This is Shiva. For Shiva is the *linga*.

Was it not this that Saul saw on the road to Damascus? this that Christ tried to get into the heads of the apostles: the smallest is me, the poorest, the most deprived, that is me?

I am Vishnu in the dwarf, the tortoise, the pig. And in Rām, the handsome warrior and Krishna the flautist and lover of cow-girls just as much as the tutor of Arjuna.

I am your coachman, your driver, if only you have a bit of common sense.

---

29. "Meher Baba": Meher Baba (1894–1969) was a spiritual master and self-proclaimed *avatāra* from Pune, India.

30. "that *avatāra* . . . a 'pig'": Varaha, the third *avatāra* of Vishnu; apparently referring to Claudel's "Pig" in *Knowing the East*?

I am your Christ, loved in the beggar who makes you miserable squawking after you, in the sergeant who drafts you as much as in the infant who gives its cheek to you for a kiss.

All this flows, flows—do you feel it?

The freight-car passing by, the train that puffs, whistles, these water supply points, these hoists, these stalls where they sell tea and bread: this is all me.

And you, you are that: *tat tvam asi*.[31]

And do you see, sin, sin is only making centers in this endless swirling movement where the water, rather than moving forward, turns, turns round on itself, the centers dragging the drops into themselves, stopping them, making them spiral to the bottom.

To the bottom: do you understand? That is hell.

But even these troubled centers do not stop the flow, for in the end these too will be carried off, though beforehand, they resisted in vain, wanting to be new centers.

That is humanity's sin: *eritis sicut Deus*.[32] But humans can only mimic God.

God is the center who is everywhere and nowhere.

And everything revolves round him, whether straight ahead, around, or even in a spiral.

Humans stop being at themselves: the ego the center of "being."

This is the Gnostics' "Demiurge." It has made air bubbles.

May 10, 1957
Pune Railway Station

---

31. "*tat tvam asi*": "you are that" (Sanskrit); Chāndogya Upanishad 6.8.7; one of the *mahāvākyas* ("great sayings") from the Upanishads.

32. "*eritis sicut Deus*": "you will be like God" (Latin); Gen 3:6.

Salvation is in accepting the complete "Otherness" of God

Salvation is in accepting the complete "Otherness" of God. An otherness whose clearest and most "unbearable," intolerable sign is Sin.

The saints have experienced this inaccessibility of God in the symbol of their sin, their incomparable agony. I can never say that I am righteous in the presence of God: the Psalmist says this when he speaks of forgotten sins, unknown sins.[33] (This reappears in the work of St. Thomas and St. John of the Cross.)

This Otherness with respect to God, in which alone I can live my original otherness I have from the Son, with regard to the Father, in which I have my being. Rising again from my death, my sin—both deaths—I will reach my status as Son.

That is, I will be.

This Otherness is the incomparable night of purification. Only in throwing oneself into this night with abandon, body and soul, can it be escaped

in the unity of being,

in my faith in Christ who is,[34] with St. Paul,

in my experience of being, with Shrī Ramana,

completely vanished as *other* and as *me*,

my non-being and my unrighteousness, my sin . . .

As long as one's distance from God remains a bearable burden, an agony possible to endure, one knows nothing.

Sin is not what the moralists say. The state of sin is to be away from God.

Is humanity not further from God in its very constitution more than in all those outward manifestations attributed to it? The book of Job testifies to this.

Even more than concupiscence, the state of original sin is manifest by the "worry," the anxiety, the dread of "possibly not being," of the uncertainty surrounding one's condition of existing.

December 12, 1959
Shāntivanam

---

33. Cf. Ps 19:8–15.
34. Cf. Col 3:3–4; Gal 2:20.

And sometimes you are called to sing

And sometimes you are called to sing that there is only One, or, rather, to sink into the endless silence of the not-two, of not-looking, of the self not even noticing the self.

And sometimes the song of unspeakable *perichoresis* rises up in your body, the self who comes to the self through the self in the manifold forms of creation,

and in this very song you become an I who rushes off to an "other" I—infinitely, the divine I who pours itself out onto itself, gathers itself up into itself.

August 14, 1963
Shāntivanam

You will only become yourself

You will only become yourself in becoming Christ.
You will never become more personally, individually, yourself, than in losing yourself in Christ.

August 18, 1963
Shāntivanam

To be one with You, Lord

To be one with You, Lord, as You are one with the Father, *in eodem Spiritu*, as you say in your farewell prayer, that through me the world might believe in You and the One who sent You.[35]

One, that Your Spirit might come into me, might fulfill his coming in me—Your work, the work of the Father, since nothing is Yours that has not come from the Father.[36] And in the unity of the Spirit, there is nothing in me that is not from You, and so from the Father.

That I might be pure manifestation for others—for the world—of You and Your Spirit, as You are pure epiphany of the Father.[37]

That is the real non-duality.

You, alone in me. Your Spirit alone in my spirit.

Your word alone in my mouth, your thought alone in my mind, your love alone in my heart.

Your prayer, your plea, my plea. Pure praise, pure love. Pure joy and the purest joy of fullness, in the peace of the Spirit.

The pure radiance of Glory.

Lord, what are You waiting for before You make real in me this non-duality, inscribed in my very origin, in the depths of Your heart, within God?

Advaita, in Christianity, is this:

—to have as a spirit only the Spirit of the Lord who acts on me to his liking, to have as a face (*personalitas*) only the person of Christ,

—to have as being only the depth of the Father's love, to find myself again in this free gift of love.

Here is true birth, receiving my new and original name.

March 30, 1964
Uttarkāshī

---

35. "*in eodem Spiritu*": "in the same Spirit" (Latin); I Cor 12:9; "that through . . . sent You": cf. John 17:21-23.

36. "the work . . . from the Father": cf. John 14:10-11 and 17:10.

37. "as You . . . the Father": see John 14:9.

I am from God

I am from God
I am in *koinonia*
My being is a gift
But precisely this gift makes me myself in this *koinonia*

April 7, 1964
Uttarkāshī

Faith is the psyche's gloaming

Faith is the psyche's gloaming, in which the basic intuition seeks to emerge, an intuition of three parts:
There is in me *aham*
There is not *nāham, anyah*
I and not-I are advaita
the *samsat* of humanity, of being.

Why must this gloaming intuition end in a particular formulation? in an acceptance of such a formulation?

A formulation of particular faith (Hindu, Jewish, Muslim, Christian) has the force of archetypal experience and all that flows into the subliminal level: myths, constellations, and confluences of myths and sociology. It gives one the possibility of being a *self*, on his own or by its choice it obliges him to make.

Faith is at root the gloaming experience that I am to be complemented by *an other who is not other*.

November 23, 1966
Uttarkāshī

In the depth of myself

In the depth of myself, the springing up of Being, the Being that in me, in my own cry, springs up of itself. God is in the very actuality that I am. There is only one *aham*. But no one will ever grasp this who is content with thinking about it.

This origin, this springing up, that haunted the Vedic poet.

Being is in itself and ever *pūrnam*. This is true.

And yet, there is, as it were, a beginning of Being when it manifests itself to the Self as *aham*.

In this *asat, pre-sat*, it springs up, so the hymns say.[38]

November 25, 1966
Uttarkāshī

---

38. "pre-sat": it appears that Swāmī Abhishiktānanda here uses the Latin prefix "pre-" (before, prior to), to modify the Sanskrit word "sat" (being). The "Vedic poet" to whom Swāmī Abhishiktānanda refers may well be the seer of Rig Veda 10.129, the so-called Nasadiya Sūkta, which speculates on the nature of creation's origins.

Jesus was pure, perfectly pure

Jesus was pure, perfectly pure. "Which of you convicts me of sin?"[39] Without trace of self-centeredness, egotism,
    completely transparent to the Father,
and so the sure and unique way to him. If this complete purity, *shuddhamātrā*, did not exist, how could one recognize impurity?

In our teaching, we dwell on the theological or dogmatic truths about Jesus. Whose formulation—all of them—is ever and terribly dependent on a given mythic environment and intrinsically relative philosophical systems.

Jesus the Yes, the Amen. He does not play, does not hide.

This transparency is his love.

Hinduism does not have a figure of such purity.

Jesus confronts the person, each person, with himself and with God at the same moment, for in his transparency Jesus is both of them at once.

This is Jesus's purity.

"Be like little children."[40]

In Jesus's clarity we have access to the Father, at the depths of the self, in the self.

Jesus the way to the self, for everyone.

Jesus the image that arises in my deepest depths and rises up in my consciousness "Who is this *yaksha*?" ask the *devas*, Indra and the others.[41]

March 15, 1967

---

39. "Which of... of sin?": John 8:46.
40. "Be like little children": cf. Matt 18:3; Mark 10:15; Luke 18:17.
41. "Who is this *yaksha*?": cf. Kena Upanishad 3.2.1–3 ff; Brahman wins a victory and the *devas* (Indra being their king) think it is their own doing, so Brahman appears before them though they do not recognize him.

I no longer saw you

I no longer saw you.
I no longer recognized you
and I lost myself.
You've taken everything:
my joy in waiting for you,
being with you.
You've escaped
in hiding yourself in my very depths,
leaving me alone
in your own solitude.

December 24, 1969
Uttarkāshī

As long as you approach Christ

As long as you approach Christ
as an other,
you haven't found him.
As long as you are content hearing his voice,
you only know without
what this voice is.
If you are the Son of God, you are the Word
of God itself
and in this word, spoken and not only
heard, you will find
and know, within, the Word.
Advaita of the Word:
vagekaivadvitīya.[42]

March 21, 1970
Feast of St. Benedict
Uttarkāshī

---

42. "*vagekaivadvitīya*": "the Word, one without a second" (Sanskrit).

See everything as Jesus did

See everything—as Jesus did—in the light of *eternity*, not of the *dvandvic mythoi*, *svarga-pātalā*, but of Being, which, in its fullness, its *pūrnam*, shines in everything.

This *Grund*, that Jesus called *Abba*.

This advaita—*not an idea*—that shines (*bhāti*) in everything, making everything luminous.

Passing beyond the limit,
beyond the *measure* that is the mind,
beyond every attempt at measuring
the beyond, which is always mythical,
beyond the name of every measure of the beyond
in that jump one is lost—*skanda*—
neither measure nor non-measure.

Jesus, not in memory but in this light, encountered *jyoti* that is *tejas*, *tapas* fulfilled in *jyoti*. Find in every being my eternal light: *nityajyoti*, the *complete* glory in the depths of all advaita: *tejas*.

Tapas: the sign of my *emergence*, that I do not let myself go with the tide.

This look that Jesus turned toward everything,
concerned but free
not unconcerned but not anxious.

March 26, 1970
Uttarkāshī

Pass through what passes

Pass through what passes,
the gaze fixed on what does not pass.

The head above the waters: death cannot reach me. Accept, like Jesus, death, and in this very acceptance reach what in me does not die, the *nitya*. To accept death is to accept the *anitya* of everything I am aware of that passes within myself—Shiva *mahākāla*—to pass to not-passing. *Passover*.[43]

March 27, 1970
Uttarkāshī

---

43. The Passover is the event described in Exod 12 when the destroying angel "passed over" the homes of the Israelites without killing their first-born sons before the flight from Egypt and the annual Jewish commemoration of God's freeing the Israelites from slavery in Egypt. Christians take the Passover typologically as a prefiguring of Christ's sacrifice in his death on the cross.

You have seen the lightning

You have seen the lightning—
keep your secret.
The lightning has torn the clouds asunder
and opened the abyss before you.
The lighting has split the heaven
you had found in your soul.
The lighting has split the firmament—
gone, the roof above you.
The lighting split your ego
and did not return.
But you know you're beyond the darkness—
keep your secret.
For those who haven't seen the lighting will think that you speak
of a fire here below.
You have seen the lighting—
keep your secret.
They would ask you to explain
and they wouldn't understand,
would condemn you.
They wouldn't understand that the heavens have been split
for you and you no longer persist beneath the firmament.
Live joyfully, smiling in the world,
endlessly free.
The heavens were split open for Jesus at his baptism[44]
and he heard the voice within.
In the split sky alone
is prayer in truth.[45]
As long as the heavens of your heart are not split
in the lightning of Sinai,[46]
the storm of Pentecost,[47]

44. Matt 3:16; Mark 1:10; Luke 3:21.
45. "prayer in truth": cf. John 4:24.
46. Exod 19:16–20:18.
47. Acts 2:1–4.

Poems from the Diary of Swāmī Abhishiktānanda

you know nothing of God,
you call God the firmament, hemmed in by thought.

. . .

Keep your secret.
You can no longer say anything, so say nothing.
No more coming down, abide in "yourself."
But who says this to me? to whom is it said?

May 9, 1970
Uttarkāshī

If there is no you

If there is no you other than myself in this moment, in this world there is no one other than me, from anywhere and everywhere it is the mystery of myself to myself that springs forth.

Before my eyes, in my ears, under my feet, at my touch, that I see, that I perceive, that I hear, that I touch, that I taste, that I reach, that I embrace.

I am that Krishna the divine eye of Arjuna gazed upon, sending forth and devouring beings.[48]

I, *aham*.

But beyond all utterance

that empties this *aham* in limiting it.

July 26, 1970
Uttarkāshī

---

48. "that Krishna ... devouring beings": see Krishna's theophany to Arjuna in *Bhagavad Gītā* 11.

Waiting for God

Waiting for God, but who is waiting? He is here: *iha* before I await him. He is the One waiting. From where, when will he come? He is Awakening itself.

Or wait for God's manifestation, wait—in time—for each moment of time. Wait for each new ray from the sun, night, day, morning, evening. Wait for the flower that blooms, the child that runs and sings, the chance look that meets my own.

An "eternal" waiting, ever filled, ever greedy. Greedy in its very fullness. Waiting without haste, without *kāma*,

to desire without desiring: *akāma, ātmakāma, āptakāma*.

Who is this Endless One, "felt" in the unique, pure experience of myself, but known—by my thought only in (not through) its manifestation in space and time?

The *theos* is not a myth. It is my temporal means of waiting for the Eternal.

To say that the *aja* alone exists and that *īshvara* is a myth, non-existent, is to make *dvandva* of Brahman *īshvara*, making Brahman disappear.

Brahman *nirvishesha* and Brahman *savishesha* are not-two. Thought is the inescapable means for living my experience of I, but it is not "other," *dvandva*, than my *ahamanubhāva*. The *theos* of prayer or adoration is not a simple projection of my thought, but the real image of the *aja* that appears on the "screen" of the world.

November 30, 1970
Advent
Uttarkāshī

Who are you, Lord?

Who are you, Lord? Do you exist? I can't go on. Are you other than this brother whose face reflects my own?

Are you some other "thing" aside from water, earth, fire, and everything made from "them"?

This *Grund* in my depths, in the depths of everything, is it a face, is it a "You" who sees itself as myself, an "I" who causes me to be in addressing me?

Are *you* other than this mystery, this Brahman, in my depths, in everything's? Listen: are you other than a simple and unspeakable mystery? This *I*, this *You*—is it a projection of myself, a final effort to preserve myself when face-to-face with you? Are you *Īshvara*? Are you *Purusha*? Are you Krishna? Are you Jesus? Are you something else, other than myself?

In that light beyond the darkness, do you still appear? Or have you disappeared in the light? Or are you this light itself surrounding me, permeating me, absorbing me?

The Logos appears only long enough to illumine the descent into the cave: the *guhā*. Then there is only left the one who is within (*guhāntara*) and who is this within himself . . .

There is no possible theology of the Spirit. *Theos*: that is the Father, the Source, the Depths, Brahman who becomes *theos* in the *logos* itself. But beyond the *logos* nothing can be said.

And true knowledge of the *logos* is in the not-professed, the not-professable of the Spirit! the Within! not any particular within, but simply the within of everything that appears . . .

In the depths of the *guhā*, there exists equally no name and no non-name, no Shiva nor Jesus!

. . .

Jesus is the mystery that *grounds* me, that *sources* me in the abyss in the *guhā* without foundation—the mystery (as we say) of the Father—and it *extends* me, *expendit*, pours me out into all that is. The Spirit, *prāna*, who makes me *antarātman sarvāntarātma*—spread throughout everything, lost in that same expansion that endlessly multiplies me as agent, in this "source-action" that reduces me endlessly, to the final identity as naught . . .

This same mystery is Jesus, who awakens me, springing up from the Father-Source and poured out in the Spirit, offered naked on the Cross, stretched out, arms extended, no withdrawal into himself, completely poured out... all gift, all Eucharistic bread, broken and given, to be given, to be eaten and become the other...

Lost in my source, lost in my fulfillment. And in this loss itself, I am...

Jesus is this mystery of advaita where I can no longer know myself *as other*. Lost as much in the *ākāsha* of the heart as in the great span of the universe, as much in the Source as in the effulgence, the radiance that empties me.

And I am Fullness, *pūrnam*, precisely in this letting-go everywhere, *sarvatra*...

And it is exactly my *pūrnam* that is the emptying of all that is me.
The *kenosis* of Christ!

December 24, 1971
Uttarkāshī

Feel in myself Jesus issuing from himself

Feel in myself Jesus issuing from himself
Feel in myself Jesus awakening to his mission
Feel in myself Jesus opening himself to his brothers
For the first reality is the intuition of myself, before every analysis of myself
Try to understand in myself that sense of the origin that he called the Father
This sense of inspiration—*ishita*—beginning in that origin that he called the Spirit.
The Spirit is that *ishanyā* from his origin, the Father, that he gives to his disciples—since he possesses it in fullness.

. . .

Jesus explodes, but nothing takes his place. This is Brahman who shines everywhere. Jesus shows us the brilliance of Brahman everywhere. He is this pure Light. There is nothing created, nothing human above him.
There is nothing above him or below him.
This whole mystery is Jesus, the *I AM, ego eimi*[49]
ahamasmi nāmakah.[50]
This final mystery is reached, naturally, through all manner of signs.
Dattātreya had 108 gurus. Every being bears the mark of every other: the smallest mite, the sand grain, the electron all shine forth from Brahman . . . And each is a way to Brahman:
ayam ātma brahma, sarvam brahma.[51]
A single cell of a living being can, theoretically, reproduce precisely this same living being.

---

49. "*ego eimi*": "I AM" (Greek); see John 4:26, 6:20, 8:24, 8:28, 8:58, 13:19, 15:1, 18:5; cf. Exod 3:14 and Rev 1:8, 1:17; translated "ego sum" in Latin.

50. "*ahamasmi namakah*": "by name, I AM" (Sanskrit).

51. "*ayam ātma brahma*": "this Self is Brahman" (Sanskrit); Māndūkya Upanishad 1.2; one of the *mahāvākyas* ("great sayings") from the Upanishads.
"*sarvam brahma*": "all is Brahman" (Sanskrit); Chāndogya Upanishad 3.14.1; one of the *mahāvākyas* ("great sayings") from the Upanishads, though the full form of this *mahāvākya* is *sarvam khalvidam brahma* ("all this is Brahman").

Jesus is not to be compared to others. No more is Krishna to be compared with others. Each is absolutely unique.

It is a false problem to see if there are several ways. The way is one because:

Brahman alone leads to Brahman—

brahmaiva brahmayanah![52]

God alone knows God.

God alone knows the mystery of Jesus, of *Purusha*, of the human person, of creation. For he alone *is* before ever there was a speck of dust!

A complete reversal of our mental perspective.

April 24, 1972
Uttarkāshī

---

52. *"brahmaiva brahmayanah"*: "Brahman leads to Brahman" (Sanskrit).

In the light of the ātman

In the light of the ātman all relations between beings (the entire giving of self to others: *annam*) are pure being, being itself, only being. Nothing to be added, nothing that can exist apart from this light. They do not differ from this light, from this being, and yet they are distinct from one another,
in the depths of the Father, the Son
in the depths of the Son, the Father
in both hands that embrace
the unique mystery of the Father and the Son.
Jesus has revealed the depths of God, of Being.

. . .

Jesus, the Spirit, is the love at the heart of all, the soul of all, the being of all, the light of all, *sarvabhūta antarātmā*, the place of beings, their *samsat*, that is their very being.
The experience of the Upanishads is true, *I know it*!
*Vedāham etam purusham mahāntam
ādityavarnam tamasah parastāt
tameva viditvā ati mrityum eti
nānya panthā vidyate'yanāya.*[53]
And I know that what I have taught in *Saccidānanda* is true, even if poorly said.[54]
The Trinity at every level,
the depth of depths,
the real of the real: *satyasya satyam* . . .
dwelling in inaccessible light.[55]

---

53. "*Vedāham etam . . . panthā vidyate'yanāya*": "I have known this great Person, effulgent like the sun, beyond darkness. Knowing him, one passes beyond death. There is no other way to pass beyond" (Sanskrit); Shvetāshvatara Upanishad 3.8 (translation drawing on transliteration and translation of Swāmī Tyagisānanda in *Shvetāshvataropanishad*, [Mylapore, Madras: Shri Ramakrishna Math, 1949], p. 66).

54. Swāmī Abhishiktānanda, *Saccidānanda*.

55. "dwelling in inaccessible light": "et lucem inhabitat inaccessibilem" (Latin); see 1 Tim 6:16.

I know, but I can only explain this knowing to *shraddhā*: Jesus could do no more: "O unbelieving people!"⁵⁶

I am.

The *mantras* where the *rishis* have enclosed the experience so it does not kill the person who reaches this interior departure.

The aspiration to *sahasrāra*, swallowed up in the heights. The *Purusha* who is its own light: *svaprakāsha!*⁵⁷ There the ātman reaches *shānta-ātma*, *samprasāda ātma*.⁵⁸ From there alone peace radiates, peace is reached.

One dies from the experience of the *ananta*,
beyond the beyond:
Brahman.
Death, death, in becoming Brahman, the ALL
Brahman *sarvam*.
Yes, this is true,
swallowed up in this Source!
The Lord said to me: I have begotten you *this day*.⁵⁹
Ah, this *tejomayah Purusha*⁶⁰
before the creation of the world
in their creation
the golden embryo
of all!
This *Purusha* in the golden embryo
who is born *aja*,
who lives in all birth.
Ah, but it is myself!
*Hiranmaya para garbha.*⁶¹
Ah, when he reveals himself,
when the sun explodes,
the world's ending:
then I am.

---

56. "O unbelieving people!": see Matt 8:26.
57. "The *Purusha* . . . own light": see Brihadāranyaka Upanishad 4.3.
58. "*shānta-ātma*": see Katha Upanishad 5.13 and Maitreya Upanishad 5.1. "*samprasāda ātma*": see Chāndogya Upanishad 8.3.4.
59. "The Lord . . . *this day*": Ps 2:8; Acts 13:33; Heb 1:5 and 5:5.
60. "*tejomayah*": see Brihadāranyaka Upanishad 2.5.1.
61. "*Hiranmaya para garbha*": "gold-colored beyond the womb" (Sanskrit); cf. Mundaka Upanishad 2.2.10.

In the Bosom of the Father

Marc and I have two bodies, two *purusha*, but the *Purusha* is one, the depths of this "trinity": *prabhavāpyayau hi ubhayah*.[62]

Jesus, Son of the living God,
have mercy on me,
in your death
save me from death,
redeem me,
Pretya to the world of light!
In this death, Jesus, save me.
This "mortal" swallowing up
in the *sahasrāra*.
Baptism of fire![63]
Saving Resurrection and Ascension!
Devastating experience of light!
Blessed are you, Father
who have brought us to yourself . . .
called to be you
called to be
called to the unborn
jyoti—sat—amritam.[64]

Shock at finding the abyss between God-Brahman and myself.

Shock at finding in the abyss that there was no abyss. The abyss is illusion! Ah! An illusion of wanting to cross over it! And Marc said to me: Even an illusion to say that there is no abyss!

Then: simply struck with panic.

May 11, 1972
Uttarkāshī

---

62. "Marc": Marc Chaduc (Swāmī Ajātānanda, 1944-____), disciple of Swāmī Abhishiktānanda (see intro).
"*prabhavāpyayau hi ubhayah*": "source and end of both" (Sanskrit).

63. See Matt 3:11; Luke 3:16.

64. "*jyoti—sat—amritam*": see Brihadāranyaka Upanishad 1.3.28.

The Trinity is a three-fold depth

The Trinity is a three-fold depth when the laser cuts to the deepest depth of my being. A three-fold depth of myself, not an idea received from outside, an abstract state, but an experience in my own consciousness that the Master's revelation still helps to formulate: *abhikliptum*.

The name of these depths: *sahatvam—vaktram—gūdham*.
Sahatvam: the mystery of the being-with, of the *relation*, of the Spirit.
Vaktram: the face manifested by the word-*vāk*, the *Purusha*.
Gūdham: the absolutely unutterable Depth, the Father.

The name of God is simultaneously revealed and hidden in the Old Testament. Yet God spoke so much in it, manifested so much of himself. Jesus claimed for himself the function of the Word and of Judgment. He gave back to God his mystery by taking on the function of God manifesting God.

God is communion—God is Word and face—God is mystery. I am communion. I am word and face—I am mystery. Each human "I" is communion, word, and face, mystery. All of creation is communion, word, and face, mystery.

Sahatvam, vaktram, gūdham.

July 3, 1972
Uttarkāshī

This experience of intimacy

This experience of intimacy, of immanence, or, rather, of non-distance (there is no "abyss"!), Jesus called "the ABBA," and India has called the *ātma-brahman, aham asmi brahman*.[65]

Jesus's *mahāvākya*:

The Lord of the heavens, but my Abba!
> *Lokeshvarah pitaiva me!*
> *Sarveshvarah pitaiva me!*
> *Svargeshvarah pitaiva me!*[66]

Abba, the mystery of non-distance!

And it is this "non-distance" with the Lord, with the One called God, Jesus gives us.

YHWH: Abba (my father).

The notion of generation is secondary to that of intimacy: does not the adopted child also have the right to say, "Abba"?

August 25, 1972
Indore

---

65. "ABBA": see Mark 14:36; Rom 8:15; Gal 4:6. *ātma-brahman*: "(this) Self is Brahman" (Sanskrit); Māndūkya Upanishad 1.2; one of the *mahāvākyas* ("great sayings") of the Upanishads (the full *mahāvākya* is *ayam ātma brahma*).

"*aham asmi brahman*": "I am Brahman" (Sanskrit); Brihadāranyaka Upanishad 1.4.10, one of the *mahāvākyas* ("great sayings") of the Upanishads.

66. "*Lokeshvarah pitaiva . . . pitaiva me*": "The Lord of the world is my Father! / The Lord of all is my Father! / The Lord of heaven is my Father!" (Sanskrit).

Poems from the Diary of Swāmī Abhishiktānanda

You are

TVAM ASI
ajātah ananta amara anādih
ekam evādvitīyah
tvatto nānyo'sti kimcit vyatiriktah
svānubhavaikapūrnahridayah
tvatto sarvam pravartate
abhayam sarvabhūtebhyo

YOU ARE
unborn, endless, deathless, beginningless
one without a second
You are not distinct from anything
the heart full of the unique experience of the self
from you everything has emerged,
no fear, love for all beings!

July 5, 1973
Rājpur

A meeting this week with very sincere preachers of Christ

A meeting this week with very sincere preachers of Christ. I didn't know what to say to them; everything it seemed I should tell them was so abstract. The obvious theme of *nāmarūpas* has no meaning for those who have not touched the depths. Lead them not to the idea or memory of Jesus, but to the present experience of Jesus as present. But those who live at the level of the *nāmarūpas* will have the experience of Jesus in his manifestations, the *nāmarūpas* of the Spirit: visions, tongues, and the rest . . .

That is all correct, but there is another level, where without words Jesus lived face-to-face with the Father and no longer named him. To this extent he was simply one who gazed at the Father,
> no longer knowing that he looks at him,
> nor that he himself is called Jesus.
> This fundamental experience of "I am"
> that removes him from all ego
> and makes him the one who is nothing more
> than a straining toward the Father, toward his human brothers.
> Gentleness, love, humility,
> zeal for the singular claim of the Absolute.

Do everything, every act *nirmāno nirahamkāra*,[67] in my love and service of Marc, of everyone, in the act of writing, of talking, . . . of eating, of buying, finding shelter, clothing . . . not as if it were another acting—for to think of oneself in the third person is still dualism—not thinking that there is only the Self, but without even the thought, in the endless freedom of the Spirit.

The need for extremes, as I had at Arunāchala and Marc has now, to "release" in oneself the call of the absolute. And we need them, these fundamental shocks of life—visions, interior experiences, external extremes, to release the *Purusha*.

And yet the *Purusha* is not in any "extreme,"
> for he has no place,
> in neither *dīkshā* nor *bhikshā*,

---

67. "*nirmāno nirahamkāra*": "without 'mine,' without ego" (Sanskrit).

nor in the Ganges.
He is. He is, when I write this, when I eat, and when I go to the bank!

July 8, 1973
Rājpur

Poems and Poetic Passages from Other Prose Sources

From "Cheminements intérieurs"

Excerpts from *Intériorité et révélation: Essais théologiques* (*Interiority and Revelation: Theological Essays*)

[p. 47]

"*Ego sum qui sum,*" *aham—aham,* Yahweh.[1] Enter within the panoply of beings from the inside, as God does.

God enters in, is within beings as

    peace, benevolence, and without a second: *shānta, shiva, advaita*
    wisdom, truth, infinity: *jnāna, satya, ananta*
    being, consciousness, bliss: *sat, cit, ānanda*

Such is God's "blessing."
Such is the blessing, *āshīrvādam,* of he who is one with God.
And like God, he offers blessing without a word.
He is and he blesses.
For, withdrawing inside himself, he is and *is* within.

[p. 71]
For, before the Father was, what could be?
and before God was,
before Being was,
before eternity?

[p. 72]
The *Father* and *I* are one . . .[2]
All that pleases *Him, I* do . . .[3]
Whatever *He* commands, *I* do . . .[4]
The Spirit that *I* send on *His* behalf . . .[5]

---

1. "*Ego sum qui sum*": "I am who am" (Latin); Exod 3:14.
2. John 10:30.
3. John 8:29.
4. Cf. John 12:50.
5. Cf. John 15:26.

In the Bosom of the Father

[p. 80]
Entering into one's own depths,
falling into one's self,
discovering in one's very depths
the secret of Arunāchala,
forever become the depths,
the incomparable Arunāchala.

March, 1953

It is, then

Excerpt from *Ermites du Saccidānanda* (*Hermits of Saccidānanda*), 81–82

 It is, then, not only in their external behavior, but also and above all in the depths of their souls—at the sacred space of the Divine Encounter, in this *guhā*, in this Interiority
>where, alone, one is before God;
>where, alone, one is with God;
>where, alone, one is in God;
>where, alone, one is from God;
>where, alone, is the One who is—

that souls consecrated to God are united by the demands of the Incarnation and their own consecration, united by the necessary bonds of their brothers, their race, their people.

March, 1953
Cave of Arutpāl Tīrtha, Arunāchala

From "Ehieh asher ehieh"

Excerpts from *Intériorité et révélation: Essais théologiques* (*Interiority and Revelation: Theological Essays*)

[p. 88]
Anima animae meae, vita vitae meae,[6]
"soul of my soul, life of my life,"
self of my self, self of every self, the Self of Self . . .
You are at the source of my "I,"
You are the source of my "I,"
You are my "I."

[p. 92]
    God is the One within everything, at the source of all, at the source of the utterance itself of the "You" I say to him.

    As long as one has not returned to the source within oneself, where otherness itself is born, one merely toys with exterior idols, made according to one's own measure:

    as long as one hasn't found the source of the self at the center of the self,
    in the source of the self, the Self in the source,
    the source in the self of being in its source.

[pp. 97–98]
    The sage does not see distinctions (*bheda*). Not only because he fixes his gaze on interior realities—*antarmukha, ātmanishtha*—but first and foremost because he is, in all things, from now on incapable of seeing anything but what is inside, this unique bosom of the unique depths, inherent to all, essential to all, in which every action inheres for the viewer—whatever aspect, whatever name he might put on for him whose eyes have not yet been opened and who can only see what is outside,

---

6. "*Anima animae . . . vitae meae*": cf. Augustine, *Confessiones*, 7.1.2.

of him who, never having turned his gaze to his interior,
has never heard resound there
the OM of the mystery and silence murmured there by Arunāchala

. . .

November–December, 1953

From "L'Epiphanie de Dieu" ("The Epiphany of God")

Excerpts from *Intériorité et révélation: Essais théologiques* (*Interiority and Revelation: Theological Essays*)

[pp. 114–16]

India's way is going beyond and going beyond the beyond, seeking Brahman, an insatiable search for being
—in an ascent reaching back in time even before time existed
—in a descent before time, after it has disappeared,
finally catching its secret,
beyond eternity too,
antequam terram faceret,[7]
ante luciferum,[8]
before the Light,
in Principio,[9]
in the mystery of originary unity, wherefrom all springs forth,
from the final unity that fulfills all
that are in the bosom of the Father at the beginning of eternity
and the Spirit, his essential end,
the Son, in his own act of procession
the manifesting-manifested,
the One who, once known, makes known
the Word welling up within, completing
within
the Fire that dispels the Darkness and destroys it,
the mystery, if you will, from the column of Fire.
The column of Fire who was Arunāchala in mythic times, the *Tejo-linga*, the sign of Flame, in which from ancient times India, in the myths of Vishnu and Brahmā, has sought unceasingly to find the foundation and summit, the Origin, the Beginning and the end,
the originary *avyakta* that is the Father,
the final *avyakta* that is the Spirit.

---

7. "*antequam terram faceret*": "before the earth was made" (Latin); Prov 8:23.
8. "*ante luciferum*": "before the daystar" (Latin); Ps 110:3.
9. "*in Principio*": "in the Beginning" (Latin); Gen 1:1; John 1:1.

And yet, is the Son knowable in himself? In truth, he is not knowable in the Father from whom he proceeds nor in the Spirit where he returns. The Son also remains unknowable, pure *avyakta*, regardless of the Father and the Spirit.

The Incarnate Word is known in the Father and is known in the Spirit. And yet—what Son? what Father? what Spirit? These are human words and human thoughts. Who has ever reached the Real by means of human thoughts?

We remain in the mystery of manifestation, in the puzzle of *māyā*, creaturely words that veil what they reveal, that hide as much as they uncover,

> the power of darkness and illumination simultaneously—
> a bright cloud.

All that is *māyā*, all that is the world, and it leads beyond itself. But it only leads the one willing to go beyond, willing, at the end of that road, to throw oneself into the abyss,

> into the Darkness,
> within the Flame ...

But what words can touch the Mystery of the Father, the originary *avyakta*,

> the mystery of the Spirit, the final *avyakta*,
> the mystery of the Son, who alone manifests the Father and the Spirit, themselves unmanifest, unable to manifest outside the Son who manifests them, whom they manifest,
> the mystery of God's Epiphany in his creation, which reached to being and the fullness of manifestation in the Spirit and in his return to the Father, in the *avyakta* that is not complete as long as it remains outside God, in whom alone it reaches its *svarūpa*, in the Spirit, *sarvasvasthatvam*,
> the mystery of the *avyakta*, the Unmanifest, who accomplishes the Epiphany,
> the mystery of the Epiphany that brings everything together in the eternal silence of the *avyakta*?

They say the Spirit is ultimately the One who manifests, the One who reveals. But is it not more precisely that in bringing the manifestation to a close, in bringing everything into the mystery of the original *avyakta*, that he brings it to perfection, that he reveals it,

> in the return to the primordial silence in the bosom of the Father,
> in the unutterable *advaita*, the unutterable non-duality?

Aren't words, you'll ask, empty rhetoric? But is it not in the play of one's words, one's thoughts, that one goes beyond words and thoughts?

[p. 118]

Is the mystery of the *avyakta* something other than the mystery of the bosom of the Father, wherefrom everything springs up and where everything returns, where everything *is*? Is it not precisely there that both the Hindu and the Christian come when they return within,
> when they enter into the depths,
> inside the *guhā*—or the *garbha*—
> into the heart of Arunāchala?

. . .

Where is the Christian? Where is the Hindu? Where is Arunāchala?

What has become of the sacred mountain?
Where have the holy pools gone?
The deep caves?

[pp. 125–26]

Neti, neti, "not this, not this," he repeats with the Brihadāranyaka Upanishad.

> Not knowable from within, nor knowable from without,
> not complete knowledge, nor unknowing,
> invisible, inapproachable,
> inexpressible, unnameable,
> such is the root of the knowledge of the unique Self
> who dissolves diversity, in which everything resolves:
> peace, bliss, beyond duality: *shāntam, shivam, advaitam*,
> the state beyond, *turīya*, [10]

---

10. "*shāntam, shivam, advaitam*": this description of the Self becomes standard in Advaita Vedānta; see Māndūkya Upanishad 7.

"Not knowable . . . beyond, *turīya*": this verse paragraph is a loose translation of Māndūkya Upanishad 7.

as the astonishing Māndūkya Upanishad says.

...

And yet, in those same words he utters, what new wonders have not bolstered his faith? This is the whole Epiphany of the Son of God in eternity and in Time, in the Trinity and the Incarnation, which he understands in the words *neti, neti* found in the Brihadāranyaka Upanishad and the apophaticism of the Māndūkya.

For the *avyakta* is the Bosom of the Father, where the Son is born.
For the *avyakta* is the incomparable Silence in which the *Vāk* resounds,
    the Word of God.
For the *avyakta* is the Darkness that springs up in the Light,
    the mystery of the Spirit who brings together all things.

And the *vyakta* is the engendering of the Son in the Bosom of the Father,
    the resounding of the Word in the Silence,
    the springing up of the Light in the Darkness,
    the fulfillment of the Epiphany in the Spirit.

The Epiphany of God is the being of God itself.

December, 1953

If this body is allowed to drop away

Excerpt from *Gnânânanda: Un maître spirituel du pays tamoul* (*Gnānānanda: A Tamil Spiritual Master*), 83–84

    If this body is allowed to drop away and this mind agrees to disappear, this is so that at last, from the original matrix finally attained, the "pure sign" the stone [Shiva *linga*] symbolizes might emerge at the center of "the place of rebirth"—every joy surpassed, every peace transcended, as the Buddha taught.

    For, so the sacred *linga* might be found standing in the depths of the cave of the heart, everything needs to be abandoned and surpassed,
>peace and the feeling of peace, and the thought itself of peace,
>joy and the thought of joy, every feeling of joy,

every thought and inner savor,
the thought and the savor of being oneself, myself,
the thought of renouncing every thought,
the savor of renouncing every savor . . .

    Then, only the lotus grows upward and flowers, its leaf touching the water but never *wet*; then the bee comes to drink its nectar.

    Vanya [Swāmī Abhishiktānanda himself] then thought too of all those devotees who so often had prostrated themselves before him, even that very evening in the *mandapa* of the temple—as if the robe he wore made *him* that sign, *linga, par excellence* of that mystery expressed at once in the glorious *linga* of fire on the summit of Arunāchala and the humble *linga* of stone hidden in the sanctuary of this village temple:

    Shiva prostrate before Shiva,
Shiva opening to Shiva his grace-filled hands,
the *līlā* of Shiva. . . .
the galaxies that turn round about one another in infinite space,
>and the electrons that play, flee, and return to one another
>>in the bosom of the atom,

>and the protons in the nucleus that split and explode,
>those who blow up the world by reuniting them—
>all that the *līlā* of Shiva and his *linga*—
>the fathers, mothers, children,

Poems and Poetic Passages from Other Prose Sources

    the different peoples,
    man become one with woman, Shiva-Pārvathī...
Then, he dreamt someone was calling his name, that he refused to speak,
that the other insisted, that finally he said:
    Who are you, you who ask my name?
    who am I, whom you ask?
    and what do you ask in this request?
    Is not everything the *līlā* of the Lord?
    you, me, and everything that we say?
    the mystery of his epiphany,
    in the very bosom of the Self,
    Shivalinga...
    OM

Shortly after March, 1956

In the Bosom of the Father

In my greatest depths

> Excerpt from *Sagesse hindoue, mystique chrétienne* (*Hindu Wisdom, Mystical Christianity*), 235

In my greatest depths, in the most hidden mirror of my heart, I tried to find the image of the One whose image I am, the One who lives and reigns in the endless space of my heart. But the reflection grew more and more pale, and soon it was lost in the original splendor. Down and down I went into what seemed to me like successive depths of my true self, my being, my consciousness of being, my bliss in being. At last there was nothing left except him, the One, Alone and endlessly alone—Being, Consciousness, Bliss, *Saccidānanda*. Within *Saccidānanda*, I had returned to my original source.

"*Tat tvam asi*—you are that," was the last thing my heart heard, and then I slept the sleep of being,[11]

ego dormivi et soporatus sum.[12]

He looked at the image
in the self,
but the image disappeared
in the Self,
and nothing remained of the look—
only What was gazed upon!

---

11. "*Tat tvam asi*": "You are That" (Sanskrit); Chāndogya Upanishad 6.8.7; one of the *mahāvākyas* ("great sayings") from the Upanishads.
"and then . . . of being": cf. next line.
12. "*ego dormivi et soporatus sum*": "I laid down and slept" (Latin); Ps 3:6.

And I also sing the OM

Excerpt from *Sagesse hindoue, mystique chrétienne* (*Hindu Wisdom, Mystical Christianity*), 254–55

And I also sing the OM. I speak the OM that rises up from the Father, that springs up in myself, that is silence in the Spirit.

And this OM that I speak, ineffably, I am it. For I, myself, this creature, this unique person, exist only in the Word of the Father, the *fiat*, the OM, of the eternal dawn.[13]

I am this OM the Father utters through the Son in the Spirit, this OM, endless going-out of God toward himself, within himself,

this OM and this *Saccidānanda*, saved from their monism and stasis, taken up in the force of the Spirit,

this *being*, this *consciousness*, this *bliss*, that are God and his most intimate expression and the deepest secret of the being of my own self,

in my communion with all things—for being is indivisible—and the incommunicability and irreducibility of my own person at once,

in the circumincession and circuminsession, the intersubjectivity of all created persons, their *koinonia* of love, in the *Pleroma* of the Son and in the Church,

in the circumincession and the circuminsession, the intersubjectivity of the Person of the Son with the Persons of the Father and the Spirit.

I sing the *Saccidānanda* of the Father, through the Son, in the Spirit. I sing the Glory of the *Saccidānanda* of the Father, through the Son, in the Spirit.

I am myself the Glory of *Saccidānanda*, in the call to being addressed to me by the Father, in the Son, through the Spirit,
    in my birth from the Glory of the Father,
    in my awakening to the Glory of the Son,
    in being nothing-but-Glory in the Glory of the Spirit,

---

13. "this *fiat* . . . eternal dawn": cf. Gen 1:3.

>in the final mystery of the OM that is "I" in the Father, when being springs up in the bosom of God,
>
>>and that in the Spirit is the SELF, when God gathers himself into himself,
>>
>>>fulfilling the divine mystery.

In the Gospel

Excerpt from *Sagesse hindoue, mystique chrétienne* (*Hindu Wisdom, Mystical Christianity*), 265

In the Gospel, Jesus did not give his disciples a method of *dhyāna*, no method of *yoga*. He simply commanded them to love.

Awakening to being in the depths of the soul does not follow from knowledge on the one hand or ascetic practice on the other. God alone can do this. Love alone is the way:

love that brings one out of oneself, leading one to his brothers and to God,

love that is as strong as death—death, which, in God's providence, is the only road to Life.[14]

---

14. "love that . . . as death": Song 8:6.

ॐ *Wholly burnt*

From a letter to Marc Chaduc (Swāmī Ajātānanda)

ॐ
Wholly burnt,
wholly risen
from the ashes!

An embrace
of one another
A kiss
that does not end
When there is no other,
who is there to kiss?
to embrace?
to encounter?

The desert:
without,
within—
the Limitless

Alone: from the Alone
Full: from the Full
Nothing: from Nothing

Tad etad vai tad[15]
That's it!

The one who feels the desert
is not the Desert—
what desert knows
it is the desert?

15. "*Tad etad vai tad*": "That, truly, is that" (Sanskrit); playing off the repeated sentence "etad vai tat" ("This, verily, is that"), throughout the Katha Upanishad.

What desert?
Who is missing?
Who deserted?

Nevertheless,
the Sign—
you need it:
you are body and blood
you are lips
you are arms and eyes!

Your ātman
is just as much your body
that eats, that drinks,
that embraces, that lives
Your ātman
is the breath that enters you,
the thought that describes you,
the joy that you are
Your joy fills everything,
your eyelashes,
the smoothness of your skin,
the damp of your lip

The Silence
ever springing forth, wherefrom is
the Word

> March 21, 1972
> Poona

Easter joy!

From a letter to Marc Chaduc (Swāmī Ajātānanda)

> Easter joy! Joy within!
> Boundless light,
> radiant in its own splendor!
> radiating eternity from Being.
> In the beginning was the Self
> in the form of *Purusha*.
> He looked, saw that Self
> and said, "I am"!
> Just so, whoever emerges from the darkness
> and finds himself in the light
> has passed into the self,
> into the unique *AHAM*.

March 29, 1972
Poona

ॐ *Dear child*

From a letter written to Marc Chaduc (Swāmī Ajātānanda)

ॐ Dear child
unborn and ever born
born from me, born from all, from water, fire
       from truth, beauty!
me in you, you in me
a serene ocean, shoreless!

May 28(?), 1972
Gyansū

In the Bosom of the Father

I wrote my monastery to say "Hallelujah"

From a letter written to Marc Chaduc (Swāmī Ajātānanda)

I wrote my monastery to say "Hallelujah." I think that you like to sing "alleluia" too—Hallelu, Yah! You see, you don't like me to speak about God, and yet you always have his name upon your lips! *Yah*! Play the game without hang-ups!

> There is a time for the mind to be silent
> a time for the body to say "Om"
> a time to sing of love—
> love that opens to uncover itself
> lips parting for the joy of meeting
> eyes glancing for the joy of seeing
> and in between, the Spirit, the non-duality of both,
> the embrace fulfilled in the silence
>   that grasps all
>   Om

April 21, 1973
Gyansū

Poems and Poetic Passages from Other Prose Sources

You a Baby?

From a letter to Marc Chaduc (Swāmī Ajātānanda)

You a baby? me a baby
in my womb? in your womb
eka eva advitīya![16]
    guhāyām parena nākam[17]

April 28, 1973
Gyansū

---

16. "*eka eva advitīya*": "there is but one without a second" (Sanskrit); an Advaitic teaching.

17. "*guhāyām parena nākam*": "beyond the heavens, in the cave (of one's heart)" (Sanskrit); adapted from the Mahānārāyana Upanishad 12.14. Swāmī Abhishiktānanda reports receiving this verse from one of Shrī Ramana Maharshi's disciples during a conversation in 1949 on his second trip to Arunāchala (*Souvenirs d'Arunâchala* (1978), 34).

OM Marc

From a letter to Marc Chaduc (Swāmī Ajātānanda)

OM

Marc

my beloved
my child
unborn:[18]
too good,
this morning of June 30
and you were too good
yourself
when we chanted our *mantras*
together
in the Ganges
when I received you in the Ganges
naked and streaming with water
like the milk
from your mother's breast
and when you left
the color of fire
alone
in the solitude of the Self
of Yourself
knowing nothing
but yourself
I envy you
I embrace
your beautiful *parivrāja* feet,
your heart,
your lips closed

18. "unborn": Marc Chaduc's *sannyāsī* name was "Swāmi Ajātānanda" ("one whose bliss is in the unborn").

Poems and Poetic Passages from Other Prose Sources

in interior silence
I hear you calling me
without ceasing:
Come, my beloved,
come your very self,
where you have sent me—
to the Source,
wherefrom no one returns!
filled with joy
of the solitary experience of being
a heart full
ekarasa!
nothing else satisfies—
arasa
nirvedam!
not food
not anything,
not work
O naked happiness!
Free from everything
Free to be yourself
Blessed *Purusha*
Unique *Hamsa*
the color of gold,
who moves freely
in the self,
his own light
svayam jyoti[19]
!

* * *

Now you are not only
my child
whom I love madly,
but you've been transfigured in my eyes
as I was in yours . . .

19. "*svayam jyoti*": "one's own light" (Sanskrit).

in you I had *darshana*
of the unborn
ajāta
OM

* * *

I pant after you
as you panted
after the Light
in the Great night
Shiva Bhairava
You are this naked beggar
at Arunāchala
aloka
parivrāja
calling me
tearing me apart
from my depths
You strip me of everything
You
Shiva Arunāchala
I have stripped you
You have stripped me
without and within
nothing but Shiva
so'ham[20]
without place, without bond
without act
a column of fire
ajāta
ananta!

* * *

---

20. "*so'ham*": "I am That" (Sanskrit); Īsha Upanishad 16; one of the *mahāvākyas* ("great sayings") of the Upanishads.

Poems and Poetic Passages from Other Prose Sources

Your *dīkshā*
like your flight from me
made me shudder
to the depths of being,
removing me to my very self,
losing myself in endless space
where I know nothing more
where I search for myself in vain
OM
*ajātānandābhishiktānandaikarasānanda
chidānandajnānānanda
ātmānandapūrnānanda
brahmānanda
ramanānandasadāshiva*[21]
OM
Like John to Jesus in the Jordan
so we came into the Ganges
Tat tvam asi // Om Abba!
Whoever was after
came before

---

21. "*ajātānandābhishiktānandaikarasānanda . . . ramanānandasadāshiva*": "the bliss of the unborn, bliss of the Anointed, the bliss of having the same object of affection, the bliss of consciousness, the bliss of knowledge, the bliss of the self, the bliss of fullness, the bliss of Brahman, the bliss of the pleasing one and the ever auspicious one" (Sanskrit). This series of Sanskrit epithets is in part a compounding conflation of names suggesting several men's spiritual intimacy in "the Self," a sort of spiritual genealogy: "Swāmī Ajātānanda" was Marc Chaduc's *sannyāsī* name; "Swāmī Abhishiktānanda" was of course Dom Henri Le Saux's *sannyāsī* name, and he was Swāmī Ajātānanda's guru; both are brought together by the "bliss of having the same object of affection." "Chidānanda" refers to Swāmī Chidānanda Sarasvatī (1916–2008), President of the Divine Life Society and the Swāmī who initiated Swāmī Ajātānanda into *sannyāsa* along with Swāmī Abhishiktānanda in Swāmī Ajātānanda's ecumenical *dīkshā*; "Gnānānanda" presumably refers to Shrī Swāmī Gnānānanda Giri (d. 1974), who had instructed Swāmī Abhishiktānanda early on during his time in India. These men, along with Shrī Ramana Maharshi ("Ramanānanda") and Sadāshiva Brahmendra ("sadāshiva"), form an intimate circle of figures with whom Swāmī Abhishiktānanda had a profound spiritual communion. While this lofty spiritual communion is obvious, one assumes that this bringing together of Swāmī Abhishiktānanda's teachers, peers, and primary disciple in this intimate way just months before his death speaks to his most cherished personal relations as well. In addition, however, given the terms "ātmānanda," "pūrnānanda," and "Brahmānanda," these relationships all point to the ultimate realization and bliss of the fullness (*pūrna*) of the Self (*Ātma*) as Brahman.

IN THE BOSOM OF THE FATHER

into the reach of infinite space—
what wondrous joy
Hamsāya namah![22]
There is no more before or after
but only the infinite and ineffable
Point
OM

* * *

In dressing you
and seeing you reclothed,
I discovered
that the *kāvi* was not only
a sign,
but a mystery
an explosion outward
of the *tejomaya purusha*,
of the depths of Being.

June 30xJuly 9, 1973
Rājpur
Upon the occasion of Swāmī Ajātānanda's *sannyāsa dīkshā*
(held June 30, 1973 in Rishikesh)

---

22. "*Hamsāya namah!*": literally, "reverence or salutation to the swan" (Sanskrit), but see glossary.

MARC

From a letter to Swāmī Ajātānanda (Marc Chaduc)

> MARC,
> Shiva's column of fire
> brushed by me
> Saturday afternoon
> at the Rishikesh bazaar
> and I still don't understand
> how it failed to carry me off
> Joy, *samprasāda*
> OM *tat sat*[23]
> *eka drishti*[24]
> *eka rishi*[25]
> Ah!
> the fulfillment.
> OM!
> I embrace you
>
> July 1x9, 1973
> Rishikesh

---

23. "*OM tat sat*": "OM, That (is) the (absolute) Being or Real" (Sanskrit); one of the *mahāvākyas*; see Shvetāshvatara Upanishad 1.16 and *Bhagavad Gītā* 17.23.
24. "*eka drishti*": "singular gaze" (Sanskrit).
25. "*eka rishi*": "unique rishi" (Sanskrit).

Now the last sign itself is over[26]

Now the last sign itself is over; the time has come for the great departure from which there is no possible return. Henceforward the guru has no right to recall his disciple.

>Go, my son, in the freedom of the Spirit,
>across the infinite space of the heart;
>go to the Source, go to the Father,
>go to the Unborn, yourself unborn,
>to the *Brahma-loka*
>which you yourself have found
>and from which there is no returning.[27]

Immediately the new *sannyāsī* sets out on his path, the path of the Self, the "ancient narrow path"[28]

>in this world, out of this world,
>seer of what is beyond sight
>he goes secretly and hidden, unknown,
>mad with the madness of those who know,
>free with the freedom of the Spirit,
>filled with essential bliss,
>established in the mystery of the non-dual,
>free from all sense of otherness,
>his heart filled with the unique experience of the Self,
>fully and for ever awake . . .

OM

ॐ

AprilxMay, 1973

---

26. These poems and the framing prose are from the form for "ecumenical" *dīkshā* composed for Marc Chaduc's *dīkshā* in April-May 1973, published posthumously in *The Further Shore* (1975), 56. These verses were apparently the only extant ones Swāmī Abhishiktānanda composed originally in English, and they were later translated into French in *Initiation à la spiritualité des Upanishads*, 230–31.

27. "to the . . . no returning": cf. Brihadāranyaka Upanishad 4.4.23 and Chāndogya Upanishad 8–end.

28. Brihadāranyaka Upanishad 4.4.8.

Afterword

IN THE BOSOM OF *the Father: The Collected Poems of a Benedictine Mystic* is a unique book in that it has the immense merit of assembling for the first time a complete collection of all the poems written by Swāmī Abhishiktānanda during the twenty-five years he lived in India. They have also been translated from the original French into English. The majority of these poems were published during his lifetime or posthumously. However, the poems found in his typewritten manuscript *Guhāntara* had remained unpublished until now.

The late Dr. Judson B. Trapnell, who authored several research papers on Swāmī Abhishiktānanda, had written to us in the early 2000's with the project of publishing a complete anthology and study of Swāmī Abhishiktānanda's poetry that would include the *Guhāntara* poems. Sadly, his tragic departure in 2003 prevented fruition of this work. He had also intended to write an additional book on the life and thought of Henri Le Saux in the form of an intellectual and spiritual biography. His untimely death was deeply regretted.

Much was our surprise when Dr. Jacob Riyeff contacted our Abhishiktānanda Centre in 2015 about his intention to write an essay on Swāmī Jī and his poems! We ardently welcomed his project and provided him with a digital copy of the unpublished *Guhāntara* poems.

We are grateful to Dr. Riyeff for having successfully completed the task of assembling all of the poems of Swāmī Abhishiktānanda into one single volume and for having beautifully translated them into English. This is a volume that has been long awaited. Also, for the first time, readers are presented with the inclusion of a remarkable collection of poems in praise of the sacred mountain Arunāchala.

In addition to composing his own poems, Swāmī Abhishiktānanda compiled the deeply inspiring devotional hymns composed by Shrī Ramana

Maharshi. He translated them from the original Tamil into French. In these hymns, the Sage expressed his overwhelming love for the Mountain, its form a manifestation of the Divine, and in which his "I" was swallowed up in the unique "I" of Shiva-Arunāchala. Within the depths of his innermost self, there was none other than the same Supreme Reality manifested in Arunāchala. These freely-translated poems of the Maharshi are also available in this volume and have been rendered into English by Dr. Riyeff with the kind permission of Shrī Ramanāshramam.

In his early poems, written directly from his heart between 1953 and 1956 and further edited in the 1960's, Swāmī Abhishiktānanda conveyed—in a symbolic way—something of the indescribable advaitic experiences which were granted to him during his extensive stays on the sacred mountain and which transcended all theological formulations. Truly, poetry has always been the supreme form of language chosen by mystics to convey their highest contemplative experience. Their poems are all born of silence and lead to the same.

As a matter of fact, this collection of poems is the crest jewel of Dr. Riyeff's anthology and expresses the profound turning point of Swāmī Abhishiktānanda's spiritual journey. This took place in January 1949, after he had received the *darshan* of Shrī Ramana Maharshi, just five months after his arrival in India. Overcoming his initial perceptions and prejudices, Swāmī Abhishiktānanda, eventually, was deeply touched by the silence and peace that emanated from Shrī Ramana in whom he "discerned the unique Sage of the eternal India."[1] This silent meeting left an immeasurable impact on his pursuit of advaita. As he wrote later in his diary: "The advaita of Ramana is my birthplace";[2] "they—Shrī Ramana and Arunāchala—have entered into my flesh, they are woven into the fibres of my heart!"[3]

However, it was only after the "Great Departure" of Shrī Ramana (April 14, 1950) that the real encounter took place, as he experienced deep states of meditation while residing on the slopes of the Mountain and there had his first great mystical insights. Later in his life, he would refer to the Mountain as his place of Awakening: "But as for myself, like Shrī Ramana, it was Arunāchala that awakened me. Oh, that Awakening!"[4]

---

1. Swāmī Abhishiktānanda, *The Secret of Arunāchala*, 9.
2. Swāmī Abhishiktānanda, *Spiritual Diary*, March 9, 1955 (unpublished).
3. Swāmī Abhishiktānanda, *Ascent to the Depth of the Heart*, 175.
4. Ibid., 354.

Afterword

It was in March 1953, while he was staying for the third time on Arunāchala, spending four weeks in the cave of Arutpāl Tīrtha, that a definitive shift took place: "[he] understood advaita and the essential pages of Guhāntara were written."[5]

The next important stage on his spiritual journey involved the meetings in December 1955 and March 1956 with Shrī Gnānānanda, a living Sage, who lived not far away from the Ramana Āshram, and whom he immediately recognized as his own master. It is with him that Swāmī Abhishiktānanda experienced the intimate relationship of guru-disciple and received confirmation of the call of the Self, this "experience of totality ... which arises from the very ground of being."[6]

From his spiritual diary, letters, and books, it can be clearly seen that Swāmī Abhishiktānanda understood the quintessence of the message of the Upanishads from the early 1950s. And yet, it took him another twenty years to realize it directly in what was to unfold as his experience of Awakening in Rishikesh in July 1973.

Strongly imbued with Christian theology, he sincerely tried, at first, to understand Advaita (Non-Duality) from a Christian point of view. Later, in the light of his deep intuitions, he reversed his approach by trying, this time, to understand the concepts of the Christian faith from Advaita. But the synthesis between the Christian dogmas and Advaita, although it was the constant object of his reflections, seemed to escape him. It was, in fact, an impossible process—to try to intellectually reconcile often incompatible philosophical categories. And yet, without the shadow of a doubt, he believed in the truth of Christ at the same time as he adhered so fully to the truth of Advaita as revealed in the Upanishads. This philosophical and existential dilemma long tormented him and his anguish and despair are well reflected in his spiritual diary, *Ascent to the Depth of the Heart*. This dilemma was later dissolved as the ultimate epilogue and came with the fire of a supreme overtaking—the Awakening to the Self—and he could finally avow: "If at all I had to give a message, it would be the message of 'Wake up, arise, remain aware' of the Katha Upanishad."[7] "And what is left for me to do in this life, apart from inviting others to make this discovery?"[8]

---

5. Ibid., 213.
6. Swāmī Abhishiktānanda, *Guru and Disciple* (2012), xxxix.
7. Stuart, *Swāmī Abhishiktānanda*, 310-11.
8. Ibid., 312.

Both Shrī H. W. L. Poonja, a direct disciple of Shrī Ramana Maharshi (named "Harilāl" in his writings, later called "Pāpājī" by his many disciples), and Shrī Gnānānanda, his guru, had warned Swāmī Abhishiktānanda against too great an attachment to intellectual research and writing, which they felt was a major obstacle preventing him from waking up.

Over the years, Swāmī Abhishiktānanda became aware that Truth is not conceptual and lies beyond all religions and conceptualizations, these being only *nāma-rūpa* (names and forms of the phenomenal world) that point to the unspeakable and inexpressible Reality.

Yet, the ultimate meeting that led Swāmī Abhishiktānanda to the direct Recognition of the Self came in October 1971. It was then that he met Marc Chaduc, "a truly total disciple,"[9] who in turn became, as it were, influential in his own Awakening.

The poems addressed by Swāmī Abhishiktānanda to his disciple have been very appropriately included by Dr. Riyeff in his anthology. They are found at the end of the compilation, as they were also the last poems written by the Swāmī prior to his Awakening. They express the intimacy of the guru-disciple relationship and, paradoxically, the impact of the transformation that took place within the disciple and upon the guru himself.

Witnessing Marc's first experience of deep absorption (*samādhi*) in God and the Absolute on May 10, 1972, Swāmī Abhishiktānanda was himself overwhelmed and said, "I now know that the Upanishad is true."[10] In the same letter, he continued, "All that I have said now seems to me off the point, so academic. . . . Neither books nor lectures can convey this experience. You have to awake to another level of awareness."

Swāmī Abhishiktānanda witnessed the rapid transformation of his disciple and his spiritual Awakening. This enhanced the process of his own Awakening which was further inspired, on the one hand, by the initiation of Marc into *vidvat sannyāsa*—the highest monastic renunciation in the Hindu tradition spontaneously taken by one who has already awakened to the Self. This was conferred by Swāmī Chidānanda along with Swāmī Abhishiktānanda in the Ganges, Rishikesh, on June 30, 1973. And, on the other hand, by a short, intensive and extraordinary retreat that followed the *dīkshā* eleven days later with Swāmī Ajātānanda (the new monastic name of Marc) held in a small temple in Rānāgal.

9. Ibid., 258.
10. Ibid., 268.

Afterword

At the end of his life, the Swāmī found himself facing a disciple with a pure heart who preceded him onto the path of realization, and of which he would say, like John the Baptist about Christ, "The one who comes after me is yet ahead of me."

It was after these two powerful events with Swāmī Ajātānanda that Swāmī Abhishiktānanda awakened in Rishikesh on July 14, 1973, at the very moment of his heart attack. Strangely enough, his Awakening came twenty years after his deepest experiences on the mountain Arunāchala and was, as it were, the completion of what had been initiated there. As he had written to Marc previously in the same year: "There has been nothing new since Arunāchala, twenty years ago."[11] This Awakening was a total explosion, a Copernican revolution. He discovered the Being, the Self, the "I Am" of Christ. "In this experience and existential knowledge," he says, "all Christology has disintegrated . . . The discovery of Christ's 'I Am' is the ruin of any Christian theology . . ."[12]

He would also write: "Anything about God or the Word in any religion, which is not based on the deep I-experience, is bound to be simply 'notion,' not existential . . . for all notions are burnt within the fire of experience. . . . I feel too much, more and more, the blazing fire of this 'I AM,' in which all notions about Christ's personality, ontology, history, etc., have disappeared. And I find his real mystery shining in every awakening man, in every *mythos* . . ."[13]

What he wanted to express by these strong words is that all concepts—useful and necessary elsewhere—were finally burned in the blazing fire of the experience of the Self deep within. He discovered then that the essence of Christianity and Vedānta is the same and, therefore, he realized the inner synthesis that was not possible for him to establish at the level of concepts.

Henri Le Saux had come to India with the belief that he was answering a missionary call, which, in fact, was the vibrant call of the Self within, and the urge to come was the recognition of his true Nature in the *guhā* (cave) of the heart. This burning, devouring inner quest is everywhere present in his poems. As Dr. Riyeff rightly writes in his Introduction (p. 15) "There is a pregnant longing for both consummation and annihilation pervading Swāmī Abhishiktānanda's poems that is a concentrated version of the same longing present in all his writings."

11. Ibid., 286.
12. Ibid., 310-11.
13. Ibid.

Through this excellent anthology of poems, Dr. Riyeff is able to convey the call of the Self, which deeply inspired the spiritual journey of Swāmī Abhishiktānanda as it unfolded from his major insights attained in Southern India beginning in the early 1950's. Through these poems, the reader will find an invitation from the heart to the Recognition of Self.

It is hoped that this message of a true spiritual master of our times will inspire spiritual seekers of all paths towards the realization of the eternal Truth.

Swāmī Ātmānanda Udāsīn

Director of the Abhishiktānanda Center
for Interreligious Dialogue, Delhi (India),
and Spiritual Head of Ajātānanda Āshram (Rishikesh)

Glossary of Foreign-language Words and Proper Names

ENTRIES ARE OF SANSKRIT words unless otherwise noted in parentheses. Because Sanskrit is an inflected language, there are several words that will vary in ending between Swāmī Abhishiktānanda's usage in his texts and the glossary entry, though the substance of the words should be clear between the two. Definitions with an "*" are taken from Swāmī Abhishiktānanda's own glossaries. Information in more detailed entries is derived from *Brill's Encyclopedia of Hinduism*, volumes 1 and 2, and *Encyclopedia of Hinduism* unless otherwise noted.

Abba: father (Aramaic)

Abhiklipta: in accordance with

Abhinna: undivided

Achala, acala: immobile; a Sanskrit word for mountain; see also "*giri*"

Advaita: literally, not-two; the doctrine of non-duality between Brahman (the absolute transcendent Principle) and Ātman (the Self); the school of thought that takes this concept as central is called Advaita Vedānta, its principle inceptor being Ādi Shankara (8th cent.)

Advaitin: an adherent of Advaita

Aham: I, myself*

Ahamanubhāva: direct experience of the ultimate "I"

Ahamtvam: state of the essential "I"*

Aja: unborn

Akāma: non-desire, absence of desire

Glossary of Foreign-language Words and Proper Names

Ākāsha: space, ether

Akhanda: indivisible*

Aloka: having no place in the world*

Amrita: immortality*

Ānanda: bliss, joy

Ananta: infinite

Anbé or *Anbu*: Love (Tamil); *Anbé Shiva*: Shiva is Love, the most precious title of Shiva among devout Tamils: "He who says Love (*Anbu*) and Shiva are two things, that one is ignorant!"*

Anitya: impermanent

Anna: food

Antarātman or *Antarātmā*: inner Self

Antarmukha: turned inwards

Anya: other*

Apara: literally, not supreme; inferior, relative

Āptakāma: all desire fulfilled

Arasa: being without flavor

Arjuna: one of the protagonists of the epic poem *Mahābhārata*; son of Indra and Kuntī; cousin to Krishna, he receives the teaching of the *Bhagavad Gītā* from Krishna on the battlefield before the Kurukshetra War

Aruna: the rose color of the sky in the rising sun; the rising sun itself*

Asat: non-being, unreality

Āshīrvāda: blessing

Asparsha: untouched*

Atharva Veda: the fourth Veda, including many chants to ward off disease and other maladies

Ātmakāma: desire for the Self

Ātman: the Self; the soul taken in its essence, independent of its intellectual or sensual faculties*

Ātmanishtha: fixed (*nishtha*) in the Self (*Ātman*)*

Glossary of Foreign-language Words and Proper Names

Ātmavidyā: Self-knowledge

Avatāra: descent of a Hindu god to the earth in a manifest form

Avyakta: in the etymological sense of "non-manifest," "invisible"; not in the particular sense that the term has received in Sāmkhya philosophy*

Bhagavad Gītā: a central Hindu religious text, the *Bhagavad Gītā* (ca. 200 BCE) is part of the great epic poem the *Mahābhārata* and recounts the religious teaching of Krishna to the warrior Arjuna

Bhagavan: Lord*

Bhairava: the name of Shiva considered in his terrifying and destructive aspect*

Bhāti: to shine

Bheda: difference, distinction

Bhikshā: the act of begging

Brahmā: the Creator of the universe; one of the classic Hindu triad comprised of Brahmā, Vishnu, and Shiva

Brahman: absolute Being*; the Supreme Principle or Reality

Brahmavidyā: sacred knowledge

Brihadāranyaka Upanishad: one of the oldest major Upanishads (ca. 700 BCE), possibly the earliest (some portions may date back to 1,500 BCE), associated with the White Yajur Veda

Buddhi: intellect

Chāndogya Upanishad: one of the oldest major Upanishads, associated with the Sāma Veda

Chidambaram: a temple in Tamil Nadu dedicated primarily to Shiva Natarāja (Tamil), literally, "the space of awareness"

Circumincession: in Trinitarian theology, the notion that each Person "is turned towards the other and is open and given to the other" (see Swāmī Abhishiktānanda, *Saccidānanda*, 125, n 5 and Congar, *I Believe in the Holy Spirit*, 37) (Latin); see "*perichoresis*"

Circuminsession: in Trinitarian theology, the notion that the Persons "are in or within each other" (see Swāmī Abhishiktānanda, *Saccidānanda*, 125, n 5 and Congar, *I Believe in the Holy* Spirit, 37) (Latin); see "perichoresis"

Glossary of Foreign-language Words and Proper Names

Cit: the pure absolute Consciousness

Dakshināmūrti: a manifestation of Shiva as the Master who teaches through silence*

Darshana: sight, coming face to face with the Real under a form accessible to humanity; can be of holy places, holy people, or philosophical*

Dattātreya: a Hindu deity thought to be an *avatāra* of the three primary Hindu deities (Brahmā, Vishnu, and Shiva), who was born to a sage, Atri, and travelled throughout the world learning the wisdom of all beings, taking them as his gurus

Deva: a Hindu deity (feminine: *devī*)

Devī Upanishad: one of the minor Upanishads, associated with the Atharva Veda

Dhyāna: contemplation or meditation, one of the "eight limbs of yoga" of Patanjali

Dīkshā: initiation (into the life of *sannyāsa*)

Dīpam: Hindu and Tamil festival, *Kārttikaī Dīpam* is celebrated when the moon is in conjunction with the Pleiades*

Dravidian: an adjective describing many of the languages and the geographical area of Southern India

Dvandva: dichotomy, pair

Ekarasa: literally, finding pleasure in only one thing or person; in the Upanishads and the Vedānta of Ādi Shankara, denotes the absolute identity experience (Ātman)

Expendit/expendere: to stretch out (even in death); to enlarge (Latin)

Fiat: "let it be done"; Mary's response to the archangel Gabriel in the Vulgate version of the Gospel of Luke 1:38 (Latin)

Ganapati: a name of Ganesha, a widely revered Hindu deity regarded as the remover of obstacles (and so invoked at the beginning of rites and events)

Garbha: womb; interior chamber; inner chamber of a Hindu temple

Giri: mountain

Giri-pradakshinā: circumambulation around a sacred mountain

Gopāla: cowherd, a name of Krishna, a manifestation of Vishnu

Glossary of Foreign-language Words and Proper Names

Grund: depths (German)

Gūdha: hidden, secret

Guhā/guhāntara: *guhā*: cave, cavern, mystically the crypt of the heart; *antara*: one who is within*

Guhācara: moving secretly in the heart

Guru: spiritual master

Hamsa: a swan as a symbol of Brahman, also an ascetic; its flight can symbolize *moksha* (liberation)

Iha: here

Īsha Upanishad: one of the primary and earliest Upanishads, associated with the White Yajur Veda

Ishanyā: impulse, inspiration

Ishita: having been moved

Īshvara: Lord

Jnāna: wisdom, direct and ultimate knowledge

Jyoti: light*

Kali-yuga: the last age (*yuga*) of the world, which we are currently in, an age of unhappiness and forgetting of the Real*

Kāma: desire

Kārttikai: the month of the Tamil calendar corresponding to mid-November to mid-December

Katha Upanishad: one of the primary and earliest Upanishads, associated with the Black Yajur Veda

Kāvi: saffron robe (traditional garb of *sannyāsīs*)

Kena Upanishad: one of the primary and earliest Upanishads, associated with the Sāma Veda

Kenosis: literally "an emptying"; in Christian theology the "self-emptying" of Christ's divine nature in the Incarnation (Greek)

Kevala: solitude, [the Absolute,] "ontological nakedness," absolute ineffability without qualification*

Koinonia: communion, joint participation (Greek)

Glossary of Foreign-language Words and Proper Names

Krishna: one of the *avatāras* (incarnations) of Vishnu; a friend and cousin of the protagonists of the epic poem *Mahābhārata*, in which he delivers the teaching of the *Bhagavad Gītā* to his cousin, the warrior Arjuna

Līlā: game, play; creation as divine sport

Linga: a sign; a characteristic mark, particularly: the cylindrical stone emblem of Shiva*

Logos: Word (Greek)

Loka: world, place

Mahākāla: great (*mahā-*) time/death (*kālā*)

Mahānārāyana Upanishad: one of the minor Upanishads, associated with the Black Yajur Veda

Maharishi: a title of respect earlier denoting the seven great rishis of the Vedas; later, a title of respect used for realized sages (like Shrī Ramana Maharshi)

Mahāvākya: great (*mahā-*) saying (*vākya*), the most important statements/insights of the Upanishads

Maitreya Upanishad: one of the minor Upanishads, associated with the Sāma Veda

Manas: mind

Mandapa: pillared pavilion

Mandira: a Hindu temple.

Māndūkya Upanishad: one of the primary Upanishads, associated with the Atharva Veda

Mantra: words or formulas repeated to aid devotion and/or meditation

Mauna Mandir: Temple of Silence

Māyā: irreality, illusion; the constantly changing apparent reality mistaken as absolute and concealing the eternal Reality

Mundaka Upanishad: one of the primary Upanishads, associated with the Atharva Veda

Mūrti: form; manifestation, and so an icon, idol*

Glossary of Foreign-language Words and Proper Names

Murugan: one of the divine "forms" most venerated in Tamil Nadu from long ago;* the son of Lord Shiva, also known as Kārttikeya; the Child God, the Beautiful God*

Naivedya: ritual offering of food*

Namah: hail, a salutation to someone

Nāmarūpa: "name and form," the phenomenal manifestation of the universe

Natarāja: an epithet of Shiva as the Lord of the Dance, the Dance of victory or the cosmic Dance

Nīlakantha: *mūrti* [or "form"] of Shiva who, at the churning of the Sea of Milk, in order to obtain *amrita* (ambrosia) swallowed poison (*nīla-kantha*: literally, "blue throat," since the poison remained in his throat)*

Nirvedam: having disgust for something, absence of interest

Nirvishesha: without distinction, undifferentiated

Nitya: eternal

Nityajyoti: eternal light

OM: the mantra of mantras from the Vedas representing the Absolute; the ineffable sacred sound and syllable through which all things were called into existence and all things return to God, their origin

Para: transcendent*

Parāmitā: ultimate*

Param-Jyoti: incomparable Light*

Parivrāja: a wandering monk, a renunciate, the fourth and final order of ascetics

Pārvathī: Hindu goddess; wife of Shiva; one of the *Tridevi* or triad of goddesses, including Lakshmī and Sarasvatī

Pātalā: inferior world, lower plane of existence

Perichoresis: patristic term for the "in-existence of the [Trinity's] Persons within each other, the fact that they are present to each other, that they contain one another and that they manifest each other" (Congar, *I Believe in the Holy* Spirit, 37) (Greek); see equivalent Latin terms "circumincession" and "circuminsession"

Perumal: a title for Vishnu (Tamil)*

Glossary of Foreign-language Words and Proper Names

Pleroma: fullness (Greek)

Prajna: knowledge of Wisdom*

Prāna: breath; spirit; vital force

Prasādam: grace; the part of a ritual offering given to the faithful*

Pretya: having departed

Pūrna: fullness

Purusha: literally "person" or "self"; in Vedic times corresponded to a "cosmic person"

Raikva: see Chāndogya Upanishad 4.1*; Raikva instructed King Jānashruti in the knowledge of Brahman

Rām(a): one of the *avatāras* of Vishnu; the protagonist of the epic poem *Rāmāyana*

Rig Veda: the first Veda (ca. 1,500 BCE), including mantras praising deities and several hymns that tell of creation

Rig, Sāma, Yajur: collections of Vedic hymns*

Rishi: Vedic seer*; a title of respect, earlier referring to the sages who saw or called forth the Vedic mantras (also called the "*maharishis*"), while later the term also referred to great sages who were not associated with the compilation of the Vedas

Saccidānanda: Absolute Being, Consciousness, and Bliss; the very essence of Brahman

Sadāshiva Brahmendra: an ascetic of the eighteenth century, whose tomb, venerated since his death, is located in Nerur near Karur on the shores of the Kāverī River*

Sahasrāra: the thousand-petaled lotus, the *cakra* (literally "wheel" or "center," subtle energy centers) at the top of the head

Sahatva: being together, communion

Sākshī: witness*

Sāma Veda: the third Veda, including mantras sung with melodies (many of which are mantras from the Rig Veda)

Samādhi: a state of total absorption that is the goal of meditation

Samprasāda: serenity

Glossary of Foreign-language Words and Proper Names

Samsāra: the world of becoming, constantly in flux*

Samsat: being together*

Sanatkumāra: one of the mind-born children of Brahmā; a rishi who instructs the rishi Nārada in the Chāndogya Upanishad and is there also called "Skanda"

Sannyāsa: renunciation*; the monastic life of contemplation, dedicated solely to the attainment of *moksha* (liberation); the fourth and final stage of the age-based life stages in Hindu tradition marked by renunciation of all worldly possessions and ties

Sannyāsī: renunciate; a person (most often a man) who has left social obligations to live a life of asceticism and has taken proper monastic initiation from his guru; in earlier times, usually a monk of the Dashanāmi Order of Ādi Shankarāchārya, consisting of ten monastic lineages

Sarva: each, every, all

Sarvabhūta: all beings

Sarvajna: all-knowing

Sarvāntarātma: the Self present in all things

Sarvasvasthatvam: you as self-abiding in everything

Sarvatra: everywhere

Sarveshvara: Lord of all

Sat: being

Satya: truth

Savishesha: with distinction

Shabda-Brahman: literally, "word-Brahman"; the Veda taken as revealed sound and associated with Brahman

Shānta: peaceful

Shānti: peace

Shānta-ātma: the self of peace

Shanmugan: six-faced; another name for Lord Murugan (Tamil)*

Shiva: etymologically, "Benevolent"*; one of the most widely worshipped deities in Hinduism; one of the classic Hindu triad comprised of Brahmā, Vishnu, and Shiva

Glossary of Foreign-language Words and Proper Names

Shraddhā: faith

Shrī Ramana Maharshi (1879-1950): one of the most celebrated sages of Swāmī Abhishiktānanda's contemporary India; born in Madurai in 1879, he was moved to spiritual life early on when a deep imaginative experience of death lead him to the recognition of the Self beyond body and mind; Self-realized at the age of sixteen, he settled for the remainder of his life on the sacred hill of Arunāchala in Tiruvannamalai; his peaceful presence attracted thousands of spiritual seekers from both East and West, to whom he primarily recommended the practice of meditative Self-enquiry (*ātma-vicāra*) through the question "Who am I?"

Shuddhamātrā: complete purity

Shvetāshvatara Upanishad: one of the principle Upanishads, associated with the Black Yajur Veda

Singheshvara: a Shaivite form of the eternal god comprised of the three great gods

Skanda: etymologically, "the Jumper"; the Son of Shiva par excellence*

Svaprakāsha: self-luminous

Svarga: a heavenly realm

Svarūpa: proper form, true nature

Swāmī: literally, "lord," "master"; a title of respect used for a renunciate, a *sannyāsi*, an ascetic in a monastic order, or a religious master; also a divine title (from Sanskrit, "svāmī")

Tapas: heat, austerity

Tejas: light, glory, fire

Tejolinga: linga of fire

Tejomaya: glorious, brilliant

Theos: God or god (Greek)

Turīya: literally, the fourth; the fourth state of (pure) consciousness that underlies and transcends the three usual states: waking consciousness, dreaming, and dreamless sleep

Udgītha: the principal chant, the essential melody of Vedic liturgies (e.g., Chāndogya Upanishad 1)*

Glossary of Foreign-language Words and Proper Names

Upanishad: a group of texts at the end of the Vedas regarded in the Hindu tradition as part of *shruti* (revelation); they comprise the core teaching of the Vedas and are referred to as "Vedānta" (the end and essence of the Veda); as religious texts, they are diverse in composition, scope, and doctrine, but the portions that have found most attention in Hindu and Western study attempt to understand the nature of the identity between Ātman and Brahman

Vāk: Voice, Word, speech*

Vaktra: face

Veda: the foundational texts of Hinduism, these *shruti* (revelation) texts were orally composed ca. 1600-600 BCE, retained in memory, and have been handed down in distinct traditions (though they have been recorded in writing for several centuries); each Veda (Rig, Yajur, Sāma, and Atharva) is comprised of four sections, *Samhitā* (including primarily the mantras or chants recited during rites), *Brāhmana* (including primarily commentary on the rites presented in the *Samhitās*), *Āranyaka* (including commentary on rites and esoteric interpretations of the Vedic rituals to be performed in the wilderness due to their power), and *Upanishad* (including, amidst a wide-ranging scope of concerns, philosophical speculation on the nature of ritual, the identity between Ātman and Brahman, and the ultimate Reality)

Vedānta: one of six orthodox Hindu philosophical systems; a school of thought founded primarily on the insights found in the Upanishads, which are also known as "Vedānta" (literally, "the end of the Veda"); centrally concerned with the relationship of Ātman and Brahman and the attainment of *moksha* (liberation from the cycle of rebirth)

Vidyā: knowledge*

Vishnu: one of the most widely worshipped deities in Hinduism; one of the classic Hindu triad comprised of Brahmā, Vishnu, and Shiva

Vyakta: manifest

Yaksha: being; spirit

YHWH: the tetragrammaton, referring to the name Yahweh, first used biblically at Gen 2:4 (Hebrew)

Yajur Veda: the second Veda, including mantras for the Vedic sacrifice (many of which are mantras from the Rig Veda rearranged for use in sacrificial settings) and comprising two recensions, the White Yajur Veda and the Black Yajur Veda

Yoga: one of six orthodox Hindu philosophical systems; also refers to a variety of religious and spiritual traditions, practices, and systems of thought in Hinduism as well as other traditions such as Buddhism and Jainism, all with the general goal of clear perception, purification of mind, and liberation (with a wide variety of answers as to how to achieve each of these states)

Appendix

The following extract is from Swāmī Abhishiktānanda's book Hindu-Christian Meeting Point: Within the Cave of the Heart, *117–19. Though his thought clearly shifted throughout his life and no one sample of his writing could do justice to the subtlety and wide-ranging nature of his insights, I have selected this brief statement of his perspective on the spiritual life as one representative example for those new to Swāmī Abhishiktānanda's work and a reference point for the content of the poems presented here.*

The end of man is the vision of God; and in order to enable him to attain this end, God gave him the capacity of knowing, which he exercises at different levels. First, there are the external senses and sense-perception. Then, at a higher level, but still depending on the senses, there is intelligence and the conceptual awareness of the self and the universe. Finally, crowning all, God has given him the possibility of a pure and non-reflexive self-awareness. In the course of evolution man has gradually been refined and has become less immersed in the matter from which God originally drew him. He has also progressively attained to new and ever higher levels of knowledge, reflection and awareness. But God chose India to lead the human spirit to the highest peak of consciousness.

Greece was chosen for a different mission. She had to provide the infant Church with the means of expressing in conceptual terms the essential message she had received from the Lord. Only thus could the faithful transmission of that message be assured until the end of time. The Church was wonderfully enriched by this osmosis of Hellenic wisdom and Biblical revelation. From age to age the Spirit of Understanding will continue to reveal to the faithful the treasures of knowledge enshrined in these formulations.

To the Vedantic experience, however, was entrusted the task of preparing for the work of the Spirit of Wisdom. Although older in time than the Greek discovery of the world of the intellect, it has been called later in history to make its contribution to the Church and so enter into the plan of salvation. This is fitting, for it opens up to the action of grace that level of the human psyche which seems to mark the culmination of all that man is capable of finding and realizing in himself. In the design of providence Vedānta is surely the ultimate preparation for the Gospel, for it disposes man to comprehend its most sublime mysteries in total lucidity.

In all this there can be no question of the Christian trying to add an impossible "something extra" to Vedānta, some transcendent truth of a higher order, or (to use the Indian term) to "superimpose" upon it anything whatever. Instead, with the help of the advaitic experience itself, he must discover and make available the fullness of the treasure contained in the experience of Christian faith. It is at this point of contact between advaita and the knowledge of faith that the Christian, himself a son in the Son, attains in the unity of the Spirit to the experience of the Father, the experience of that Glory which Jesus both promised and communicated to his own. Naturally this will mean, first of all, a personal experience of being a child of the Father, a creature, a reconciled sinner. But, beyond and in the depths of this basic experience of being a son of the Father, he will also share in the very experience of the Father himself, his joy and bliss, since in virtue of being his son and heir, he has a right to share in all the Father's goods. If one may dare to express it so, it is the Father's experience which alone is eternal life and the principle and source of all that is and all that lives. It is by the communication of this experience which is imparted to me, in the communion that I have with God who is my own Father and the Father of our Lord Jesus Christ, that I myself receive being and life. But this communion with the Father is beyond all duality of thought. It is only in the experience of Being at its very source, in the awakening of Being to itself, that I stammeringly utter my response of love to the eternal appeal of the Father's love. Or rather he utters it in me when he utters it in his own Word, in the very act by which he is himself.

Here there is certainly an ineffable "I" and "Thou"; but there is also, simultaneously and inseparably, a non-duality, *ekatvam*, that is no less ineffable. Only an awareness of this *ekatvam*, the unity of the Spirit, gives access to the mystery of the communion of love which is at the heart of that unity. And it is the Spirit of Wisdom, the divine *Pneuma* in the depths of our own *pneuma*, who makes us experientially aware of this through a connatural knowledge. This indivisible mystery of *koinonia* (communion) and *ekatvam* (non-duality) is universally present in being—between the divine Persons, between men, between men and God. But it is most perfectly revealed on earth in Jesus, the Man-God, since the whole fullness of the divine Being, the Godhead, is bodily present in his very flesh (Col 2:9). Communion in non-duality, unity in self-communication—such is the law of being.

The final secret is the bosom of the Father, which is prefigured in the Upanishadic symbol of the *guhā* (cave), the most inward recess of man's heart and at the same time the furthest and loftiest heavenly abode, as the Taittiriya Upanishad (2.1) says, speaking of Brahman: *nihitam guhāyām parame vyoman*. It is the mystery which is inaccessible in its very proximity, close at hand and yet transcendent, at once both interior and exterior, and yet not reducible to terms of within and without, "beyond all things," as the Īsha Upanishad reminds us. But the Father reveals the inmost secret of his nature only to those whom he has chosen (cp. Katha Upanishad, 2.23) in Jesus Christ (Eph. 1:4), the Word made flesh, the One who, as God and as man, is the essential and unique Revelation and Epiphany of the Father.

Books by Swāmī Abhishiktānanda
(chronologically in English)

An Indian Benedictine Ashram. With Jules Monchanin. Shāntivanam, Tannirpalli, 1951. Reprint: *A Benedictine Ashram*, Douglas: Times Press, 1964.

Swami Parama Arubi Anandam: Fr. J. Monchanin (1895–1957). Shāntivanam, Tannirpalli: 1959.

The Mountain of the Lord: Pilgrimage to Gangotri. Bangalore: CISRS, 1966. Reprint: Madras: CLS, 1967. New and revised edition: Delhi: ISPCK, 1990.

Prayer. Delhi: ISPCK, 1967. New and enlarged edition: 1989. Reprint: Philadelphia: Westminster, 1973. Reprint: London: Canterbury, 2006. Revised and enlarged edition: *Prayer: Exploring Contemplative Prayer through Eastern and Western Spirituality.* Edited by Swāmī Ātmānanda Udāsīn. Delhi: ISPCK, 2015.

Hindu-Christian Meeting Point: Within the Cave of the Heart. Bombay: IIC/Bangalore: CISRS, 1969. Revised edition: Delhi: ISPCK, 1976. Reprint:1997.

The Church in India: An Essay in Christian Self-Criticism. Madras: CLS, 1969. Reprint: 1971.

Towards the Renewal of the Indian Church. Bangalore: Dharmaram College, 1970. Reprint: 1971.

Guru and Disciple: An Encounter with Srī Gnānānanda, a Contemporary Spiritual Master. London: SPCK, 1974. Revised edition: Delhi: ISPCK, 1990. Reprint: 2000. New and enlarged edition: Edited by Swāmī Ātmānanda Udāsīn. Chennai: Samata Books, 2012.

Saccidānanda: A Christian Approach to Advaitic Experience. Delhi: ISPCK, 1974. New edition: 1984. Reprint: 1997.

Books by Swāmī Abhishiktānanda

The Further Shore. Delhi: ISPCK, 1975. Reprint with addition of *The Upanishads and the Advaitic Experience* and poems: 1984. Reprint: 1997.

The Secret of Arunāchala: A Christian Hermit on Shiva's Holy Mountain. Delhi: ISPCK, 1979. Reprint: 1988. Revised edition: 1997.

In Spirit and Truth. Delhi: ISPCK, 1989. Reprint: 2000.

The Eyes of Light. Denville, NJ: Dimension Books, 1983.

Ascent to the Depth of the Heart: The Spiritual Diary (1948–1973) of Swāmī Abhishiktānanda. Edited with introduction and notes by Raimon Panikkar. Translated by David Fleming and James Stuart. Delhi: ISPCK, 1998.

Bibliography

John Paul II. *Fides et Ratio.* Vatican City, Italy: Libreria Editrice Vaticana, 1998. Accessed November 15, 2017. http://w2.vatican.va/content/john-paul-ii/en/encyclicals/documents/hf_jp-ii_enc_14091998_fides-et-ratio.html

Mahieu-De Praetere, Marthe. *Kurisumala: Francis Mahieu Acharya, a pioneer of Christian Monasticism in India.* Translated by Susan Van Winkle. Kalamazoo, MI: Cistercian Publications, 2007.

Panikkar, Raimundo. "Foreword." In Shirley du Boulay, *The Cave of the Heart: The Life of Swāmī Abhishiktānanda,* xi–xvii. Maryknoll: Orbis Books, 2005.

———. "Introduction." In *Ascent to the Depth of the Heart: The Spiritual Diary (1948–1973) of Swāmī Abhishiktānanda (Dom Henri Le Saux),* edited by Raimon Panikkar, translated by David Fleming and James Stewart, xiii–xxxi. Delhi: ISPCK, 1998.

Paul VI. "Declaration on the Relation of the Church to Non-Christian Religions." Vatican City, Italy: Libreria Editrice Vaticana, 1965. Accessed September 8, 2016. http://www.vatican.va/archive/hist_councils/ii_vatican_council/documents/vat-ii_decl_19651028_nostra-aetate_en.html

Roebuck, Valerie, trans. *The Upanishads.* New York: Penguin, 2004.

Stuart, James, ed. *Swāmī Abhishiktānanda: His Life Told through his Letters.* Delhi: ISPCK, 1989.

Swāmī Abhishiktānanda. *Ascent to the Depth of the Heart: The Spirit Diary (1948–1973) of Swāmī Abhishiktānanda (Dom Henri Le Saux).* Translated by David Fleming and James Stuart. Delhi: ISPCK, 1998.

———. *Eveil à soi – éveil à Dieu: Essai sur la prière.* Paris: Centurion, 1971.

———. *The Eyes of Light.* Denville, NJ: Dimension Books, 1983.

———. *The Further Shore.* Delhi: ISPCK, 1975. Revised and expanded edition, 1984.

———. *Gnânânanda: Un maître spiritual du pays tamoul.* Chambéry, France: Présence, 1970.

———. *Initiation à la spiritualité des Upanishads.* Sisteron, France: Présence, 1979.

———. *Intériorité et révélation: Essais théologiques.* Sisteron, France: Présence,1982.

———. *La montée au fond du couer.* Paris: O.E.I.L., 1986.

———. *Prayer.* Delhi: ISPCK, 1967. Revised and enlarged edition,1989. Revised and enlarged edition, 2015.

———. *Saccidānanda: A Christian Approach to Advaitic Experience.* Delhi: ISPCK, 1974. New edition, 1984.

———. *Sagesse hindoue, mystique chrétienne. Du Védanta à la Trinité.* Paris: Éditions de Centurion, 1965.

———. *The Secret of Arunāchala: A Christian Hermit on Shiva's Holy Mountain.* Delhi: ISPCK, 1979; reprinted 1988. Revised edition, 1997.

———. *Souvenirs d'Arunâchala: Récit d'un ermite chrétien en terre hindoue.* Paris: Epi, 1978.

Bibliography

Adi Shankara. *Atmashatkam*. Foreword author's personal file.
Augustine. *Confessiones*. Edited by Lucas Verheijen. Turnhout: Brepols, 1981.
Baumer-Despeigne, Odette. "The Spiritual Way of Henri Le Saux (Swami Abhishiktananda): Unedited Texts." *Bulletin of Monastic Interreligious Dialogue* 48 (October 1993) 20–25.
Benedict XVI. "General Audience." May 14, 2008. Vatican City, Italy: Libreria Editrice Vaticana, 2008. Accessed November 15, 2017. http://www.vatican.va/roman_curia/congregations/cfaith/documents/rc_con_cfaith_doc_19891015_meditazione-cristiana_en.html#top
Blée, Fabrice. *The Third Desert: The Story of Monastic Interreligious Dialogue*. Collegeville, MN: Liturgical Press, 2011.
Brill's Encyclopedia of Hinduism. 6 vols. Boston: Brill, 2009-2015.
Cassian, John. *Conferences*. Translated by Colm Luibheid. Mahwah, NJ: Paulist Press, 1985.
Claudel, Paul. *The East I Know*. Translated by Teresa Frances and William Rose Benet. New Haven: Yale University Press, 1914.
Congar, Yves M. J. *I Believe in the Holy Spirit*. Vol. 3. Translated by David Smith. New York: Seabury, 1983.
Congregation for the Doctrine of the Faith. "Letter to the Bishops of the Catholic Church on Some Aspects of Christian Meditation." October 15, 1989. Vatican City, Italy: Libreria Editrice Vaticana, 1989. Accessed November 15, 2017. http://www.vatican.va/roman_curia/congregations/cfaith/documents/rc_con_cfaith_doc_19891015_meditazione-cristiana_en.html#top
du Boulay, Shirley. *The Cave of the Heart: The Life of Swami Abhishiktananda*. Maryknoll: Orbis Books, 2005.
Encyclopedia of Hinduism. New York: Facts on File, 2007.
Francis Acharya. *Cistercian Spirituality: An Ashram Perspective*. Edited by Michael Casey. Kalamazoo, MI: Cistercian Publications, 2011.
Gregory the Great. *Dialogues*. Edited and translated by Adalbert de Vogüé. 3 vols. Paris: Le Cerf, 1978-1980.
Griffiths, Bede. "Our Founders." In *Saccidananda: A Garland of Letters*, 6–9. Tiruchirappalli, India: Saccidananda Ashram, 1990.
John of the Cross. "Spiritual Canticle." In *The Collected Works of St. John of the Cross*, translated by Kieran Kavanaugh, OCD, 459–630. Washington, D.C.: Institute of Carmelite Publications, 1991.

Further Reading
(in English)

For a much fuller list, see the Bibliography on the Abhishiktānanda Centre for Interreligious Dialogue's website (abhishiktananda.org.in).

du Boulay, Shirley. *The Cave of the Heart: The Life of Swāmī Abhishiktānanda*. Maryknoll: Orbis Books, 2005.

Rogers, Murray and David Barton. *Abhishiktananda: A Memoir of Dom Henri Le Saux*. Oxford: SLG Publications, 2003.

Skudlarek, William, ed. *God's Harp String: The Life and Legacy of the Benedictine Monk Swāmī Abhishiktānanda*. Brooklyn, NY: Lantern Books, 2010.

Skudlarek, William and Bettina Bäumer, eds. *Witness to the Fullness of Light: The Vision and Relevance of the Benedictine Monk Swāmī Abhishiktānanda*. Brooklyn, NY: Lantern Books, 2011.

Stuart, James. *Swāmī Abhishiktānanda: His Life Told through his Letters*. Delhi: ISPCK, 1989; new edition in 1995; reprinted in 2000.